Ed Moll sets out to convince the reader that the doctrine of the Ascension is nothing less than biblical, Anglican and essential and this he does with admirable concision and force. It is indeed curious that the doctrine has apparently faded from its rightful place, eclipsed, perhaps, by the resurrection. But Moll has done the church a great service surveying the relevant literature (such as it is) and history. His comments are judicious and instincts reliable. We can only hope that this contribution will go a long way towards rectifying the situation.

Mark Meynell, writer and teacher, former Director (Europe & Caribbean) Langham Preaching.

The latest volume in the Latimer Trust's Christian Doctrine series is Ed Moll's study of the Ascension. Moll's intention is show that 'the ascension is an evangelical doctrine, rooted in biblical cosmology, securing our Christology, accompanying the resurrection, celebrated by the church and amply attested by the Scriptures.' His book achieves these aims magnificently. It is a must read for all students of theology, and for anyone who wants to understand Christian doctrine more clearly and expound it more faithfully.

Martin Davie is a lay Anglican theologian who is theological consultant for the Church of England Evangelical Council and a Latimer Research Fellow.

Ed Moll has given us an extensive and masterly summary of the passages in Scripture that refer to the Ascension of Jesus and, more importantly, the passages that depend upon it. In doing so, he has demonstrated that the Ascension is not a doctrinal add-on to be celebrated mid-week once a year, but is fundamental to our faith as Christian believers and should permeate every aspect of our life, liturgy and preaching. This is essential reading for all Anglicans seeking to be rooted and grounded in Biblical truth.

Revd Ian Lewis, Chair and Director of the South West Gospel Partnership.

THE ASCENSION OF CHRIST

PIONEER, PRIEST AND KING

ED MOLL

The Latimer Trust

The Ascension of Christ: Pioneer, Priest and King © Ed Moll 2024. All rights reserved.
ISBN 978-1-916834-10-1 Published by the Latimer Trust February 2025.

The Latimer Trust (formerly Latimer House, Oxford) is a conservative Evangelical research organisation within the Church of England, whose main aim is to promote the history and theology of Anglicanism as understood by those in the Reformed tradition. Interested readers are welcome to consult its website for further details of its many activities.

The Latimer Trust
London N14 4PS UK
Registered Charity: 1084337
Company Number: 4104465
www.latimertrust.org
administrator@latimertrust.org

Views expressed in works published by The Latimer Trust are those of the authors and do not necessarily represent the official position of The Latimer Trust.

Scripture quotations are from the Holy Bible, New International Version®, NIV® Copyright ©1973, 1978, 1984, 2011 by Biblica, Inc.® Used by permission. All rights reserved worldwide.

Contents

Foreword to the Christian Doctrine Series	1
1. A neglected doctrine?	5
2. New Testament Witnesses: the Gospels and Acts	11
3. New Testament Witnesses: the Letters	33
4. Anglican Witnesses to the Ascension	53
5. Doctrinal and Pastoral Connection	69
Appendix: Preaching Illustrations	93
Select bibliography	101

Foreword to the Christian Doctrine Series

What does the Anglican Church teach? What should Anglicans believe? The Anglican Communion has a reputation for tolerating a wide variety of different viewpoints, so much so that it is easy to forget that there is a core of teaching, or doctrine, which Anglicans are expected to teach and believe. Most of that core is shared with other Christians to a greater or lesser extent, but there is often a distinctive way in which Anglicans relate to that common heritage and adapt it for their own mission as witnesses to Jesus Christ in the world.

There are many good studies of Anglican doctrine available, and some of them give detailed accounts for the benefit of students and theologians from other churches. Unfortunately, there is relatively little material that addresses the needs and concerns of ordinary churchgoers, many of whom have only a sketchy awareness of the Church's teaching and are baffled by an academic approach and technical terminology that they find hard to understand. The aim of this series is to present the doctrine of the Anglican Church, and in particular of the Church of England, in a format that is user friendly and that does not assume any prior knowledge of the subject. It cannot be exhaustive, but it aims to be reasonably comprehensive and to give readers a clear sense of what the Anglican Church stands for.

Anglicans do not claim to be a special kind of Christians, distinguished from others by peculiar beliefs that set them apart from the wider Christian world. On the contrary, Anglicans claim that what we believe is 'basic Christianity' as the late John Stott put it in a book that he wrote on the subject, or 'mere Christianity' as C. S. Lewis described it in a similar volume. Anglicans adhere to the mainstream of Christian belief as this has been handed down through the centuries, and members of other Churches will find much in our heritage with which they can agree. That is as it should be, and we hope that where we take a different position to that of some other Christians, that we do so in a spirit of love and respect for them and their witness alongside our own.

In the course of time, Anglicans have rejected what they regard as aberrations in the teachings of some other Churches, and especially of the Roman Catholic Church, from which we separated at the time of the Reformation in the sixteenth century. We think that some of their doctrines have obscured the pure message of Christ and imposed beliefs that have no basis in the Bible, which is the supreme source of our faith. On other matters of controversy among Christians, Anglicans have either taken a moderate position that has tried to reconcile differences as much as possible, or else has remained silent, allowing Church members the freedom to have their own opinions without making them part of its essential beliefs. The booklets in this Series will deal with these questions and explain why Anglicans think the way they do, without condemning or dismissing the views of those who differ from us on questions where views other than our own can be defended from the Holy Scriptures that we share in common.

The aim of this Series is to guide readers through the various aspects of the Church's doctrine, avoiding technical terms as much as possible, and explaining them clearly when that is necessary. Readers who want to pursue particular subjects further are provided with a list of publications that will help them deepen their knowledge and understanding.

It is the hope of the Latimer Trust that this Series will awaken an interest among Church members in Christian beliefs that will stimulate their minds and help them grow in their faith. The Series aims to lay a foundation for the vital task of explaining what Anglicans teach and believe in a way that can be communicated positively and accurately to the wider world. It is our hope that preachers and pastors will find in it a clear presentation of the message of Jesus Christ that will guide them in their ministerial task as they proclaim the Good News of salvation to their people. May God bless them as they labour for him, and may he use the tools this Series provides for his glory and for the upbuilding of his Church.

Gerald Bray
Series Editor

1. A Neglected Doctrine?

The firework wobbled its way into the light of an early summer evening, paused and wobbled its way back to earth, spent. 'Is that it?'

As an occasion, the Celebration for Ascension Day had so much potential: a gathering of staff and students from Christian theological colleges across the city together with their families to celebrate this festival in the church's year. For many of us evangelicals, it was the first time we had attended a celebration on Ascension Day. It left me deeply underwhelmed. It made me believe that even if liberal or Catholic-minded Christians found something to celebrate in the ascension of Christ, it wasn't for me. I have spent the past decades recovering from that mistake.

How could a Bible-believing Christian come to such a conclusion? Why was I not alone among evangelicals in neglecting the ascension? I can think of half a dozen plausible reasons:

Only two Bible passages (or three)

First, only two verses, Luke 24:51 and Acts 1:9 – or three if you include Mark 16:19 – describe the ascension. If the ascension is so important, why do the New Testament writers not give more space to describing it?

Unfamiliar with liturgy

Second, the ascension is mentioned in the liturgy that we have in the prayer book, and Ascensiontide has two Collects. But low-church evangelicals may not be that familiar with either the church year or the Collects. I certainly wasn't (and to a large extent I still am not).

Not many of us echo Bernard of Clairvaux's description of the ascension as 'the consummation and fulfilment of [all] the other festivals, and a happy ending to the whole journey of the Son of God'.

Eclipsed by the resurrection

The New Testament speaks clearly of the death *and resurrection* of Christ. Paul gives extended space to expounding the death and resurrection, but no corresponding space is given to expounding the ascension. When Paul reports the faith of the Thessalonian Church in Jesus who is in heaven, he describes Christ as *risen* rather than *ascended*: 'how you turned to God from idols to serve the living and true God, and to wait for his Son from heaven, *whom he raised from the dead* – Jesus, who rescues us from the coming wrath' (1 Thess 1:9–10, my emphasis). Even the Article that affirms the ascension, Article 4, is entitled 'Of the Resurrection', not 'Of the Resurrection and Ascension of Christ'.

Just as a star becomes invisible in daylight so the doctrine of the ascension is obscured by the brighter light of the resurrection. Oliver O'Donovan agrees that:

> Contemporary theology has suffered from a tendency to ignore the ascension of Christ, no doubt out of a sense of the cosmological questions it raises as well as out of a once-fashionable tendency to discount the witness of Saint Luke and Saint John in favour of that of Saint Mark. Consequently the resurrection has borne the whole

weight of the 'forward-looking' emphasis on the exaltation of Christ, so that correspondingly its 'backward-looking' significance as the return of Christ from the dead has been lost sight of.[1]

Sum of other doctrines

As a doctrine, the ascension works by bringing together several other doctrines. We will see how this can be a strength – a good grasp of the ascension can strengthen our grasp of Christology. But if our grasp of doctrine and our confidence in affirming it are shaky, our hold on the ascension and its significance will suffer. I was raised in churches and training settings that emphasise right handling of biblical texts and prize expository preaching and biblical theology in the context of a 'Bible Overview'. I am still committed to these activities but I fear that my training in those skills came at the expense of a proper respect for doctrine in the sense of systematic theology. We never 'just teach the Bible': we always teach with and from doctrinal commitments, whether they are acknowledged or not. Without explicit attention to our doctrine, we are liable to carry significant gaps. My grasp of the ascension was one of those gaps. If this is your tribe too, then I hope that this book will persuade you that the ascension is taught in the New Testament and that it can be taught in church without compromising your commitment to expository ministry. I would go further and say that this doctrine must be taught if you are committed to teaching the Bible.

---

[1] Oliver O'Donovan, *Resurrection and Moral Order: An Outline of Evangelical Ethics* (Leicester: Apollos, 1994), 57.

Apologetically weird

A further reason why we might not teach about the ascension is that it is, frankly, weird. It is apologetically awkward when we think about where Jesus is supposed to have gone. The ascension, writes Douglas Farrow, 'is something of an embarrassment in the age of the telescope and the space probe; indeed, of evolutionary theory and faith in global progress.'[2]

It is obvious that Jesus 'went up' (the clue is in the name) but where did he go? Where is 'heaven' to which Jesus has gone if it is not within this creation? Preachers already have to contend with the scandal of the cross (how can one man's death change my life?) and the outrage of the resurrection ('dead people don't rise to new life'). We do so willingly because we are convinced of the power of the gospel about Jesus who 'was delivered over to death for our sins and was raised to life for our justification' (Rom 4:25). We are hardly likely to relish engaging with the metaphysics of the ascension if we are not even convinced it is that big a deal.

A bit Catholic

A final objection to the ascension might be that it's a 'bit Catholic'. Certainly my experience of seeing the ascension celebrated by Christians of other traditions (liberal and Catholic) and hardly hearing it mentioned within my evangelical church circles tempted me to believe that the ascension is not something that Bible-believing Christians should celebrate. We will see that while the New Testament makes little of the ascension

---

2 Douglas B. Farrow, *Ascension Theology*, (London: Bloomsbury Publishing, 2011) 16.

as an event to *describe* (in other words, Jesus' ascent), we depend every day of our Christian lives on the fact of the ascension of Christ to heaven.[3] The ascension is not someone else's special interest: it is a truth for us.

But rather

My aim in this little book is to persuade you that the ascension is biblical, Anglican and essential. The following two chapters survey and group the New Testament texts that mention the ascension, in order to give lie to the assertion that the ascension is hardly mentioned. Chapter 4 examines the witness of the Church of England's Formularies to show how Anglican liturgy expresses the ascension. Chapter 5 draws together the doctrinal and pastoral connections. An appendix gathers illustrations which may be helpful in preaching.

In this way I hope to show that the ascension is an evangelical doctrine, rooted in biblical cosmology, securing our Christology, accompanying the resurrection, celebrated by the church and amply attested by the Scriptures. I hope to inspire you to celebrate the ascension of Christ with confidence and joy.

---

[3] See Drake's Folly in the appendix for an illustration of this idea.

2. New Testament Witnesses: the Gospels and Acts

When we speak of the ascension of Christ we mean both his ascent to heaven and his ministry when seated at the right hand of the Father, known as the 'session'. In this section we will survey the New Testament passages that speak of the ascension and session.

The ascent

Luke's narrative (Luke 24:50–51 and Acts 1:9)

The ascent of Christ is narrated by Luke and forms the hinge between his two volumes:

> When [Jesus] had led them out to the vicinity of Bethany, he lifted up his hands and blessed them. While he was blessing them, he left them and was taken up into heaven. (Luke 24:50–51)

> After he said this, he was taken up before their very eyes, and a cloud hid him from their sight. (Acts 1:9)

The ascent of Jesus into heaven marks the transition of Jesus' ministry from earth to heaven. Jesus' earthly ministry stretches from his incarnation to his ascension and during that time he was active on the earth as fully God and fully man. When he ascended into heaven, he did not retire or cease to be active and he continues to be active from heaven. Luke's Gospel records Jesus' earthly ministry as 'all that Jesus began to do and to teach' (Acts 1:1); the book of Acts describes what Jesus *continues* to do from heaven.

Jesus' ascent was not a reversal of the incarnation in which the second person of the Trinity sheds his human nature to return to heaven as he was before: Jesus ascended to heaven as a man, albeit a glorified and risen human being, but as a human being on behalf of human beings. The angels' reassurance that 'This same Jesus, who has been taken from you into heaven, will come back in the same way you have seen him go into heaven' (Acts 1:11) promises that the glorified man Jesus Christ will return to earth as he left it: visibly and bodily.

Mark's narrative (Mark 16:14–20)

Mark 16:14–20 includes a description of the ascent; 'After the Lord Jesus had spoken to them, he was taken up into heaven and he sat at the right hand of God' (Mark 16:19) and is the appointed reading for Ascension Day in the *Book of Common Prayer*.

Although these verses are present in a variety of documents, some of them ancient, textual scholar Bruce Metzger considers them to be secondary, based on internal evidence. He adds that 'all these features indicate that the section was added by someone who knew a form of Mark which ended abruptly with verse 8 and who wished to provide a more appropriate conclusion.'[1] While these verses were included in the main text of the Authorised Version of the Bible, they are now considered to be a later addition and are found

---

[1] Bruce M. Metzger, *The Text of the New Testament: Its Transmission, Corruption, and Restoration* (Oxford University Press, USA, 1992), 227.

in the margin of modern translations accompanied by a footnote such as the NIV's: 'The earliest manuscripts and some other ancient witnesses do not have verses 9–20.' For our purposes we can note that these verses do not contribute anything that is not already present in the accounts of Luke and Matthew.

The passages that narrate the ascent offer only minimal commentary. However, the New Testament as a whole rests on the *fact* of the ascent and explains its importance. The following survey will reveal the main themes developed around the ascension – in other words, the ascent and the session of Jesus in heaven.

We will see that the Synoptic Gospels present Jesus as the King in heaven and that his ascent is to be a source of great joy for the disciples. The fourth Gospel introduces Jesus as the Son whose return to the Father leads through suffering to glory. It is from glory that the ascended Son and the Father send the Holy Spirit, through whom the disciples will do greater things even than those witnessed during Jesus' earthly ministry. Finally we will survey the evidence in Acts that Jesus continues to be active from heaven after his ascension.

The Synoptic Gospels: Ascended as king

The Synoptic Gospels' presentation of Jesus' ascension majors on his identity as king seated in heaven.

Ascent to Jerusalem (Luke 9:51)

> As the time approached for him to be taken up to heaven, Jesus resolutely set out for Jerusalem. (Luke 9:51)

We mentioned that Jesus' ascent into heaven forms

the canonical hinge between the two volumes of Luke's account of Jesus' ministry. Jesus' ascent into *heaven* is prefigured by Jesus' ascent to *Jerusalem* which marks a turning point in Luke's account of Jesus' earthly ministry. The road to Jerusalem was described as being 'up' in the same way that a traveller in Britain would go 'up' to London.

The Son of Man seated on his throne (Matthew 19:28)

Matthew's Gospel does not describe the ascent of Christ in the same way as Luke–Acts because Matthew's main type is Moses, rather than David. Although he also mentions Jesus' royal pedigree, Matthew reveals Jesus as the law-giver by structuring the Gospel around five teaching blocks that echo the five books of the Law.[2] That would be why, as Douglas Farrow notes, '[Matthew's] version of the story concludes with Jesus on a mountain somewhere on the fringe of the promised land, blessing and commissioning his disciples as Moses once blessed Joshua and the leaders of the tribes.'[3]

The ascended Christ is also mentioned earlier in the main body of Matthew's Gospel. In response to Jesus' teaching that 'it is easier for a camel to go through the eye of a needle than for someone who is rich to enter the kingdom of God' (Matt 19:24), the astonished disciples wonder how this can be and what reward there will be for those who have left everything to follow Jesus. We

---

[2] The five discourses are: the Sermon on the Mount (Matthew 5–7), the discourse on mission (Matthew 10), the parables of the kingdom (Matthew 13), teaching on church life (Matthew 18) and the Olivet discourse (Matthew 24–25, although some interpreters some start at Matthew 23:1).

[3] Farrow, *Ascension Theology*, 8.

are familiar with the promise that follows:

> And everyone who has left houses or brothers or sisters or father or mother or wife or children or fields for my sake will receive a hundred times as much and will inherit eternal life. (Matt 19:29)

We often miss the preceding verse which declares who has authority to reward his loyal followers in this way: the Son of Man seated on his throne.

> Jesus said to them, 'Truly I tell you, at the renewal of all things, when the Son of Man sits on his glorious throne, you who have followed me will also sit on twelve thrones, judging the twelve tribes of Israel.' (Matt 19:28)

The Son of Man who will be revealed on the last day as being seated on his throne will have been seated on his throne before then – at his ascension.

Seated in heavenly glory (Matthew 24:30, 34)

> Then will appear the sign of the Son of Man in heaven. And then all the peoples of the earth will mourn when they see the Son of Man coming on the clouds of heaven, with power and great glory. (Matt 24:30)

Jesus' teaching replies to the disciples' question about the destruction of the temple: 'when will this happen, and what will be the sign of your coming and of the end of the age?' (Matt 24:3). While what follows could be understood as a description of what will be seen later and at the return of Jesus, it is better understood to refer to the coming age. That time will be marked by wars and rumours of wars, and will come in the lifetime of those listening to Jesus, according to verse 34: 'Truly I tell you, this generation will certainly not pass away until all these things have happened.' The coming age for the disciples is the present age for us, in which Jesus is ascended and seated on his throne. Verse 30 refers to Jesus' present session in heaven (rather than to his future return from heaven).[4]

Seated at God's right hand (Mark 14:62 and Matthew 26:64, also Luke 22:69)

When Jesus is challenged by the high priest to confirm whether or not he is the Messiah, the Son of the Blessed One (Mark 14:61), he replies:

> 'I am,' said Jesus. 'And you will see the Son of Man sitting at the right hand of the Mighty One and coming on the clouds of heaven.' (Mark 14:62)

Jesus' claim combines the 'one like a son of man' of Daniel's vision who receives 'authority, glory and sovereign power' (Dan 7:13–14) with David's prophecy in Psalm 110 that 'The LORD says to my lord: "Sit at my right hand until I make your enemies a footstool for your feet."' (Psalm 110:1). Jesus often applied the phrase 'Son of Man' to himself, deliberately (in my

---

[4] The 2011 NIV footnotes link to Daniel 7:13–14, which refer to Jesus' ascension rather than his return. See below on Mark 14:62.

view) exploiting the ambiguity of a phrase that also simply means 'human being'. Son of Man is used in this latter sense over 90 times in Ezekiel. But before the high priest, Jesus' reference is unmistakably to the exalted figure. The reaction of his accusers shows that the reference is not lost on them:

> 'If you are the Messiah,' they said, 'tell us.'
>
> Jesus answered, 'If I tell you, you will not believe me, and if I asked you, you would not answer. But from now on, the Son of Man will be seated at the right hand of the mighty God.'
>
> They all asked, 'Are you then the Son of God?'
>
> He replied, 'You say that I am.'
>
> Then they said, 'Why do we need any more testimony? We have heard it from his own lips.' (Luke 22:67–71)

The Jewish leaders saw Jesus' reply as a claim to belong in glory at the right hand of the Father and they reacted with fury to what they saw as blasphemy. Jesus' claim before the council is consistent with his previous comments about himself as the Son of Man, that is the ascended King.

Path of suffering to glory (Luke 24:26)

> Did not the Messiah have to suffer
> these things and then enter his glory?
> (Luke 24:26)

When Jesus appeared to his disciples, he reassured them that he was not a ghost (Luke 24:37–39), ate with them, and then opened the Scriptures to show that, 'This is what is written: The Messiah will suffer and rise from the dead on the third day, and repentance for the forgiveness of sins will be preached in his name to all nations, beginning at Jerusalem' (Luke 24:46–47). Earlier in the same chapter, Jesus had walked with the two disciples on the road to Emmaus: 'And beginning with Moses and all the Prophets, he explained to them what was said in all the Scriptures concerning himself' (Luke 24:27). Although they had not at that point even understood the significance of Jesus being *raised*, he chides them for their lack of faith that he would *enter his glory*, that is, ascend and be seated in heaven.

All authority granted to Christ (Matthew 28:18)

> Then Jesus came to them and
> said, 'All authority in heaven and
> on earth has been given to me.'
> (Matt 28:18)

Matthew's Gospel does not record Jesus' ascent but the great commission depends on it. Jesus is the one like a Son of Man of Daniel's vision to whom is given all authority (Dan 7:13–14). He reigns because he is king, and he is king because he has ascended. Patrick Schreiner puts it in these terms: 'Certainly, Jesus had authority on the earth: he forgave sin and overpowered demonic forces. But at his ascent Jesus received power over the whole cosmos and was installed as the king of both heaven and earth.'[5] Jesus lives because he is risen but he reigns because he is ascended: 'The Ascension is primarily a Christological event declaring that, whereas the Resurrection means Jesus lives, the Ascension asserts that he reigns.'[6]

Filled with great joy (Luke 24:52)

> While he was blessing them, he left them and was taken up into heaven. Then they worshipped him and returned to Jerusalem with great joy. (Luke 24:51–52)

For the Synoptic Gospels, Jesus' ascension marks his installation as king, and this is a source of great joy.[7] Mark's Gospel had begun with the 'good news' of a new king: the ascension proclaims him to be Jesus Christ, crucified, risen from the dead and ascended into glory, to reign as king. His authority now is the authority of the risen, ascended and glorified king.

John's Gospel: Going to the Father

John's presentation of Jesus' ascension as a return to the Father introduces also the gift of the Spirit through whom the disciples will see greater works.

---

5 Patrick Schreiner, *The Ascension of Christ: Recovering a Neglected Doctrine* (Bellingham WA: Lexham Press, 2020), 89.
6 B. K. Donne, *Christ Ascended* (Exeter: Paternoster Press, 1983), 31.
7 We will see below from John 14:28 that Jesus going to the Father was also to be a source of gladness for the disciples.

There are more than a dozen references to Jesus' ascension in the fourth Gospel which may be grouped as follows:

Vision of greater things (John 1:51)

> He then added, 'Very truly I tell you, you will see "heaven open, and the angels of God ascending and descending on" the Son of Man.'

Nathanael is so impressed that Jesus knew him while he was still under the fig-tree that he confesses, 'you are the Son of God; you are the king of Israel.' (John 1:48–49). Jesus replies that Nathanael will see 'greater things' than that when he sees the Son of Man in heaven. The allusion is to Jacob's vision of a ladder in Genesis 28, and the fulfilment comes in Jesus' ascension when the Son of Man is seated in heaven and the disciples will both see and do the 'greater things' that Jesus promises in John 14–16.

Authority of the Son of Man (John 3:13, 6:62 and 5:27)

Jesus' claim to be a *teacher* with authority rests on his identity as one who has come from heaven to speak of heaven:

> I have spoken to you of earthly things and you do not believe; how then will you believe if I speak of heavenly things? No one has ever gone into heaven except the one who came from heaven – the Son of Man. (John 3:12–13)

Implicit in Jesus' claim to have come from heaven is

the assumption that he will return to heaven: in other words that he will ascend.

Jesus' authority as *king* is asserted by the feeding miracle in John 6 which the crowd misinterpret when they seek to make him king by force (John 6:15). The long discourse that follows discourages the disciples who find it to be a 'hard teaching' (John 6:60). Jesus has not come to be popular: he has come to be king. He came from heaven and will return to heaven for this:

> Aware that his disciples were grumbling about this, Jesus said to them, 'Does this offend you? Then what if you see the Son of Man ascend to where he was before!' (John 6:61–62)

Jesus' authority as *judge* is asserted in John 5:27

> And he has given him authority to
> judge because he is the Son of Man.

In the context, the Son of Man has authority to call the dead to life. While the connection is not made as explicit in John's Gospel, the Synoptics have already made the case that Jesus' coming authority is the authority of the ascended king.

Glory through suffering (John 13–16)

Before the ascension can lead to Jesus' glory, betrayal will lead to his humiliation on the cross. The path to glory lies through suffering. Even as he promised his ascension to glory, Jesus foreknew the betrayer:

> 'Yet there are some of you who do not believe.' For Jesus had known from the beginning which of them did not believe and who would betray him. (John 6:64)

John's introduction to the upper room discourse links the betrayal of Jesus with his ascension, and his ascension with a return to the Father:

> The evening meal was in progress, and the devil had already prompted Judas, the son of Simon Iscariot, to betray Jesus. Jesus knew that the Father had put all things under his power, and that he had come from God and was returning to God. (John 13:2–3)

In the Last Supper, Jesus prepares the disciples for the time when he will be taken away from them. His being taken away could refer to his death, or to his ascension, or to both. In his death Jesus was taken away and in our own experience, death separates us from loved ones. The disciples received Jesus back at his resurrection, but only for a short time. In his ascension, Jesus was again taken away from them – once again, only for a time. Jesus' departure is to prepare a place for the disciples and if his departure refers to his death, then it would be to prepare a place for them among the dead. His departure refers to his ascension because he goes to heaven to prepare a place for his disciples in heaven. He comes back to them when the promised Holy Spirit comes. The 'going away' that Jesus speaks of is his ascension to heaven and that path leads through the cross and resurrection but does not end there.

John connects his departure from the world with his return to the Father:

> I came from the Father and entered the world; now I am leaving the world and going back to the Father. (John 16:28)

For Jesus, the route from this world to the Father in heaven must lead through death but the place that he has prepared for his followers is directly with the Father in heaven *because* Jesus died and defeated the power of death.

Promise of the Holy Spirit (John 14–16)

Two blessings are promised in connection with Jesus' return to the Father: first he promises the Holy Spirit who will come *because* Jesus ascends to the Father:

> I will not leave you as orphans; I will come to you. Before long, the world will not see me anymore, but you will see me. Because I live, you also will live. On that day you will realise that I am in my Father, and you are in me, and I am in you. (John 14:18–20)

Notice that although Jesus is speaking of the Holy Spirit, he says *I* will come to you. The Spirit will mediate the presence of Jesus who is absent from the world because he has returned to the Father. More than that, the Spirit will unite us to Jesus as Jesus is united to the Father (verse 20). Jesus must go to the Father in order for the Spirit to come:

> But very truly I tell you, it is for your
> good that I am going away. Unless I
> go away, the Advocate will not come
> to you; but if I go, I will send him to
> you. (John 16:7)

The ministry of the Spirit is to bring conviction about sin and righteousness and judgment (verse 8) 'because I am going to the Father, where you can see me no longer' (John 16:10).

The disciples ask again about Jesus' leaving and then returning to them (John 16:16–18) and Jesus once again explains that his departure is to go to the Father, and that this will bring them joy:

> So with you: Now is your time of
> grief, but I will see you again and
> you will rejoice, and no one will take
> away your joy. (John 16:22)

It is tempting to identify the disciples' joy at seeing Jesus with the resurrection appearances but that would be incomplete. Jesus speaks of his return to the Father and of the sending of the Spirit, which come about in his ascension. Jesus' resurrection is only the first part of the whole movement of his ascension:

> I came from the Father and entered
> the world; now I am leaving the
> world and going back to the Father.
> (John 16:28)

The ministry of the Spirit depends on the ministry of the ascended Jesus:

- The Spirit is sent by the ascended Jesus (as we also see in Acts 2).

- The Spirit is an advocate who is with the disciples. While he is another *like* Jesus – 'And I will ask the Father, and he will give you another advocate' (John 14:16) – he is not the same as Jesus. He is sent by Jesus to be with the disciples – 'When the Advocate comes, whom I will send to you from the Father' (John 15:26).

- We have two advocates with the Father: the Spirit who is with us (John 14:16) and Jesus in heaven who is before the Father ('if anybody does sin, we have an advocate with the Father – Jesus Christ, the Righteous One' (1 John 2:1). The advocacy of the Spirit with us on earth depends on the advocacy of Jesus with the Father in heaven.

Promise of greater works (John 14:12)

Jesus' second promise flowing from his ascension and the gift of the Spirit is that the disciples will do greater works *because* he has ascended to the Father:

> Very truly I tell you, whoever believes in me will do the works I have been doing, and they will do even greater things than these, because I am going to the Father. (John 14:12)

Griffith Thomas explains that 'On Earth, their Master was necessarily limited and circumscribed, but at the right hand of God authority and power were his, and the disciples could therefore depend upon His presence and grace in all the work He was sending them to do.'⁸ Griffith Thomas cites Mark 16:20 in support: 'Then the disciples went out and preached everywhere, and the Lord worked with them and confirmed his word by the signs that accompanied it.' Even if this verse is not original to the Gospel of Mark, it is true from elsewhere that the disciples took the gospel message everywhere. The worldwide spread of the gospel about Jesus is a greater work possible only through the ministry of the Spirit, available only because of the ascension of Jesus to be with his Father. 'The presence and power of the comforter,' writes Griffith Thomas, 'led to the accomplishment of spiritual results of marvellous extent and influence'.⁹ He quotes John 7:37–39 in support:

> On the last and greatest day of the festival, Jesus stood and said in a loud voice, 'Let anyone who is thirsty come to me and drink. Whoever believes in me, as Scripture has said, rivers of living water will flow from within them.' By this he meant the Spirit, whom those who believed in him were later to receive. Up to that time the Spirit had not been given, since Jesus had not yet been glorified. (John 7:37–39)

No wonder Jesus taught the disciples that the time of his ascension would be a time of joy (John 14:28, see also Luke 24:52), and that he urged Mary not to

---

8 W. H. Griffith Thomas, *The Principles of Theology: An Introduction to the Thirty-Nine Articles* (Vine Books Ltd, 1930), 82–83.

9 Thomas, *Principles of Theology*, 83.

hold him up when she met him in the garden on the morning of his resurrection and clung to him:

> Jesus said, 'Do not hold on to me, for I have not yet ascended to the Father. Go instead to my brothers and tell them, "I am ascending to my Father and your Father, to my God and your God."' (John 20:17)

Acts: the Acts of the ascended Jesus

The ascended Christ is active throughout the book of Acts.

What Jesus began and continued to do (Luke–Acts)

Luke–Acts is a single work in two volumes with the same author (Luke) and the same main agent (Jesus). Luke tells us that his Gospel recounted 'all that Jesus *began* to do and to teach' (Acts 1:1, emphasis added) which implies that the second volume, Acts, is going to be about what Jesus is continuing to do and teach; therefore the 'Acts of the Risen Lord Jesus' would be a better title'.[10] This is a surprise if we expect the alternative title to be the 'Acts of the Holy Spirit' since the Spirit is poured out at Pentecost and is at work throughout the early church. The Holy Spirit is indeed poured out and is indeed at work, but not in order to replace Jesus as if the Saviour had retired to heaven to hang up his boots. The risen Jesus is ascended into heaven whence he continues to direct the church, which is empowered

---

10   Alan J. Thompson, *The Acts of the Risen Lord Jesus* (Apollos, 2011), 49.

by the Holy Spirit. The book of Acts tells of what *Jesus* continued to do and teach.

Even before the Day of Pentecost had come, the disciples sought a replacement apostle to fill the space left vacant by Judas the betrayer. Peter called the church together and declared that 'it is necessary to choose one of the men who have been with us the whole time the Lord Jesus was living among us' (Acts 1:21). The church prayed and asked *the Lord* to show them whom *he* had chosen (verse 24). After praying, they cast lots, echoing an Old Testament method of seeking God's leading. In this way, Matthias was not chosen by the church or even by the Spirit, but directly by the ascended Lord. The church does not resort to casting lots again because (in my view) the Lord leads directly through the Holy Spirit who speaks to the church or acts to open and close doors of ministry in response to prayer. Since we too serve the same ascended Lord, we seek his guidance through counsel and prayer and not through the casting of lots.

Jesus' exaltation and the day of Pentecost (Acts 2)

On the day of Pentecost, the Holy Spirit was poured out on the crowd of believers and Peter preached a sermon (Acts 2:14–39), the longest reported speech in Acts. We expect the sermon to be about the Holy Spirit and are perhaps surprised to find that Peter speaks mainly about Jesus. Important as the coming of the Spirit is for the church and for the world, the burden of Peter's sermon is what the coming of the Spirit *on earth* tells us about events *in heaven*. 'News of this coronation in heaven (still hidden from view) has reached earth in the pandemonium of Pentecost.'[11] The coming of the Spirit on earth confirms that we are now in the Last Days, the final lap of salvation history spoken of by the prophet Joel (Acts 2:16–21, citing Joel 2:28–32). In the Last Days, the Spirit of God is no longer restricted to some among God's people: he is poured out on all God's people, young and old, male and female. The Spirit of God is poured out like this *because* the promised king is now seated on his throne and the central section of Peter's sermon expounds Jesus' resurrection from the dead and exaltation in heaven (Acts 2:22–35).[12]

A second consequence of Jesus' exaltation beside the pouring out of the Spirit is that those who opposed, betrayed and killed him now have a reckoning to face: 'Therefore let all Israel be assured of this: God has made this Jesus, whom you crucified, both Lord and Messiah' (Acts 2:36). The coming of the Spirit confirms to these Jews that instead of serving God by getting rid of Jesus, they have opposed God. Those who see this are understandably 'cut to the heart' (verse 37).

The third consequence is that because Jesus is the crucified, risen and exalted king, there is forgiveness in his name. Those who repent of their sin and trust in Jesus as their king will be forgiven and added to the church. The statement that 'about three thousand *were added* to their number that day' (Acts 2:41, emphasis added) *may* be a divine passive: the ambiguity is cleared up by the end of the chapter which states that '*the Lord* added to their number daily those who were being

---

[11] Douglas Farrow, *Ascension and Ecclesia: On the Significance of the Ascension for Ecclesiology and Christian Cosmology* (Edinburgh, T & T Clark Ltd, 1999), 25.
[12] We saw the connection between Jesus' ascension and the sending of the Spirit in John 13–16 above.

saved' (Acts 2:47, emphasis added).

The ascended Jesus heals the lame beggar (Acts 3)

In the next chapter, Luke narrates how Peter heals a man who was lame from birth (Acts 3:1–10) and gives an explanation to the crowd (Acts 3:11–26). Once again the remarkable feature of the speech is that it does not address the main question of how *Peter* healed the man, because it was *Jesus* who healed him. That was already hinted at by Peter's words to the man, 'Silver or gold I do not have, but what I do have I give you. In the name of Jesus Christ of Nazareth, walk' (Acts 3:6). Peter's explanation is that the man was healed because Jesus is ascended: 'The God of Abraham, Isaac and Jacob, the God of our fathers, has glorified his servant Jesus' (Acts 3:13a). Peter goes on to recite how Jesus was rejected, crucified and then raised. That he also has the ascension in mind is clear: 'Heaven must receive him until the time comes for God to restore everything, as he promised long ago through his holy prophets' (Acts 3:21). The ascended Jesus is not retired in heaven but active: 'When God raised up his servant, he sent him first to you to bless you by turning each of you from your wicked ways' (Acts 3:26). The ascended Jesus is responsible both for the blessing of healing the man and for the call to repentance that follows. These are the acts of the ascended Lord Jesus.

The ascended Lord and his church (Acts 5:31–32, 7:54–56, Acts 9–23)

There are multiple examples in Acts of Jesus the ascended Lord being active in the life of the church. The ascension of Jesus is linked to *Jesus'* preaching by the persecuted apostles: 'God exalted him to his own right hand as Prince and Saviour that *he* might bring Israel to repentance and forgive their sins' (Acts 5:31, emphasis added). The Spirit and the church are active agents in Jesus' work of building the church: 'We are witnesses of these things, and so is the Holy Spirit, whom God has given to those who obey him.' (Acts 5:32).

When Stephen bore witness to Jesus before the Sanhedrin, they were furious and gnashed their teeth at him (Acts 7:54). Luke continues, 'But Stephen, full of the Holy Spirit, looked up to heaven and saw the glory of God, and Jesus standing at the right hand of God. "Look," he said, "I see heaven open and the Son of Man standing at the right hand of God"' (Acts 7:55–56). The ascended Jesus stands to receive the first martyr.[13]

Jesus himself appeared to Saul of Tarsus, the persecutor of the church who, it turns out, was persecuting *Jesus* (Acts 9:5, 8:1).

In the persecution that followed Stephen's death, some of the believers were scattered as far as Antioch. Those of their number who spread the gospel to Greeks told of the risen Lord Jesus, but it was *the Lord* who gave fruit to their mission: 'The Lord's hand was with them, and a great number of people believed and turned to the Lord' (Acts 11:21). It is the Spirit of Jesus who leads Paul into Macedonia (Acts 16:6–10), where the Spirit is called the Holy Spirit (verse 6), the Spirit of Jesus (verse 7) and God (verse 10). When Lydia hears the message, it is *the Lord* who opens her heart (Acts 16:14). It is *the Lord* who speaks to Paul in a vision about Corinth in Acts 18:9–11 and in the face of persecution

---

13   Thomas, *Principles of Theology*, 83.

in Acts 23:11.[14] Christ is ascended but active, absent but not inactive.

The testimony of Acts is that Jesus who ascended into heaven continues to lead his church from heaven.

---

[14] For most of these examples, see Chapter 1 in Thompson, *Acts of the Risen Lord Jesus*.

3. New Testament Witnesses: the Letters

Hebrews: Jesus going through the heavens

The letter to the Hebrews is an extended reflection on the ascension of Christ the Great High Priest and its significance for Christian believers. Because the ascension is foregrounded, the resurrection is somewhat eclipsed: there is only one reference to the resurrection of Christ, whom God brought back from the dead through the blood of the eternal covenant (Heb 13:20). It is the ascension that is the main truth.

Seated at the right hand

The letter's opening refers to Christ ascended and seated 'at the right hand of the Majesty in heaven' (Heb 1:3; also 8:1, 10:12, 12:2; Eph 1:20, Col 3:1, 1 Pet 3:22), which echoes the ascension references in the Synoptic Gospels and Acts to Jesus' ascension as king. The main thrust of Hebrews is to expound Jesus' ascension as the great high priest who has gone through the heavens. For a king, the right hand is the place of greatest honour, and the seat is the place from which to reign. Priests would offer sacrifices while standing and being seated implies that the offering of sacrifice is done; intercession can be done from a seated position. The ascended Jesus is seated at the right hand of God in heaven both to rule as king and to intercede as priest on the basis of a finished sacrifice.

Jesus our ascended high priest

Jesus' ascension into heaven fulfilled the pattern laid out by the Levitical priesthood in the earthly tabernacle. The death of the sacrificial victim was necessary but atonement was not complete until the sacrifice was *offered* and intercession made by the priest who went through the curtains into the Holy Place. In the same way, the death of Christ is necessary because 'It is impossible for the blood of bulls and goats to take away sins' (Heb 10:4). However, Christ's priestly work was not complete until the sacrifice was *offered* and intercession made when Jesus the great high priest went through the heavens. The focus of Hebrews is less on the death of Christ than on his ascension into heaven. The ascension is the main truth.

The argument proceeds by drawing the parallels between the Levitical priests who offer sacrifices in the earthly tabernacle and Christ's ministry in heaven in order to demonstrate how the first was a shadow pointing forward to the reality that is fulfilled in Jesus.

> • The Levitical priests are chosen from among the people they represent and 'For this reason he [the Son] had to be made like them, fully human in every way, in order that he might become a merciful and faithful high priest in service to God, and that he might make atonement for the sins of the people' (Heb 2:17).

> • The priests ministered in the tabernacle which was 'a copy and shadow of what is in heaven' (Heb 8:5a). That is why Moses was given such careful instructions about its layout (Exod 25–30 and 35–

40). Jesus, however, entered the real sanctuary of heaven itself: 'But when Christ came as high priest of the good things that are now already here, he went through the greater and more perfect tabernacle that is not made with human hands, that is to say, is not a part of this creation' (Heb 9:11).

• The priests offered the animal sacrifices prescribed by the Law to make atonement and to make holy. But these sacrifices can only bring outward cleansing (Heb 9:13) and the blood of bulls and goats cannot take away sins (Heb 10:4). Christ, however, 'entered the Most Holy Place once for all by his own blood, so obtaining eternal redemption' (Heb 9:12b).

• The priests continually offered sacrifices. Their work was never done because their sanctuary was a mere shadow. Christ enters the true sanctuary, once only:

> For Christ did not enter a sanctuary made with human hands that was only a copy of the true one; he entered heaven itself, now to appear for us in God's presence. Nor did he enter heaven to offer himself again and again, the way the high priest enters the Most Holy Place every year with blood that is not his own. (Heb 9:24–25)

• The priests made intercession behind the curtain, on the basis of the sacrifice that they took in with them. Their work was seen to be achieved when the priest emerged from the curtain a second time – until the following year, of course. And when that priest died, another had to be appointed. It is not so with Christ. Like Melchizedek who is 'Without father or mother, without genealogy, without beginning of days or end of life' (Heb 7:3), Christ is a priest forever. Christ's offering of himself does not ever need to be repeated because he was 'was sacrificed once to take away the sins of many' (Heb 9:28a). He remains behind the curtain to make intercession for he has no need to re-emerge as the earthly priests did. At his return in glory, 'he will appear a second time, not to bear sin, but to bring salvation to those who are waiting for him' (Heb 9:28b).

In his ascension into heaven, Christ the great high priest enters the true sanctuary bearing the true sacrifice to make the true offering. His work of offering done, he remains in heaven, seated to make intercession. The offering of Christ at the cross is essential but atonement is only fully achieved and the benefits fully realised for us by his ascension *into heaven:* When Christ had made purification for sins, he sat down *in heaven* (Heb 1:3); we have a great high priest who has ascended *into heaven* (Heb 4:14); we have a high priest who sat down at the right hand of the throne of the Majesty *in heaven* (Heb 8:1); Christ entered heaven itself, not a human copy (Heb 9:24–25).

While he remains in heaven, seated at the right hand, Christ is making intercession for his people and standing as a pledge of the redemption of their bodies.

The confidence that comes from Jesus' intercession in heaven

Because of Christ's intercession in heaven, we have confidence and comfort before God. These flow from Jesus' *ascension* as priest:

> Therefore, since we have a great high priest who has ascended into heaven, Jesus the Son of God, let us hold firmly to the faith we profess. For we do not have a high priest who is unable to feel sympathy with our weaknesses, but we have one who has been tempted in every way, just as we are – yet he did not sin. Let us then approach God's throne of grace with confidence, so that we may receive mercy and find grace to help us in our time of need. (Heb 4:14–16)

Our confidence is rooted in the priest who has ascended into heaven. He is able to make atonement for us and he is able to understand what we face. Both are possible because he was like us in every way (Heb 2:14–18) and yet without sin. It seems that Hebrews was written to Christian believers who were losing their own confidence that Christ, whom they could not see, was sufficient to give them access to God. They were drifting back to more tangible modes of religion. The writer to the Hebrews urges his readers to hold on to the riches that are theirs and ours in Christ:

> Therefore, brothers and sisters, since we have confidence to enter the Most Holy Place by the blood of Jesus, by

> a new and living way opened for us through the curtain, that is, his body, and since we have a great priest over the house of God, let us draw near to God with a sincere heart and with the full assurance that faith brings, having our hearts sprinkled to cleanse us from a guilty conscience and having our bodies washed with pure water. (Heb 10:19–22)

Once again we see how that confidence is rooted in the ministry of Christ the ascended priest who has gone through the curtain. The writer to the Hebrews urges his readers to make use of this confidence to draw near: 'Let us then approach God's throne of grace with confidence, so that we may receive mercy and find grace to help us in our time of need' (Heb 4:16). But he also encourages them to hold on to this confidence: 'And we are [God's] house, if indeed we hold firmly to our confidence and the hope in which we glory' and 'do not throw away your confidence; it will be richly rewarded' (Heb 3:6, 10:35).

Our confidence is rooted in Christ who remains seated at the right hand until his return in glory. That is why Hebrews affirms that 'he is able to save completely those who come to God through him, because he always lives to intercede for them' (Heb 7:25). Calvin comments that 'Having entered a sanctuary not made with hands, he appears before the Father's face as our constant advocate and intercessor. Thus he turns the Father's eyes to his own righteousness to avert his gaze from our sins.'[1]

---

[1] John Calvin, *Institutes*, 2.16.16. All references to and quotations from Calvin's *Institutes* are from John Calvin,

As F F Bruce notes, Jesus' intercession from the right hand of God connects his work as priest and as king:

> The priesthood of Christ ... began immediately after his death, when he was raised to his present supremacy. This is the moment envisaged in the oracle of Psalm 110:1, 'Sit at my right hand, till I make your enemies a footstool.' It is equally the moment envisaged in the companion oracle of Psalm 110:4, 'You are a priest for after the order of Melchizedek.'[2]

Griffith Thomas concurs that 'It was at the Ascension that our Lord entered upon His work as Priest and King and this is why the doctrinal position of the Epistle to the Hebrews centres in the fact of the Ascension in relation to our Lord's priesthood.'[3]

Finally, our confidence is rooted in the finished sacrifice of Christ. Neither Christ in heaven nor priests on earth need to repeat his sacrifice. It is done once for all. Seated, Christ is still at work to intercede on the basis of what he has offered. Donne explains, 'The act of sacrifice is over, but *The Sacrifice*, Christ himself, forever remains, in the way that with the Old Testament sacrifices, the blood stood on the altar after the victim had been slain.'[4]

Institutes of the Christian Religion, trans. Ford Lewis Battles (Philadelphia: Westminster John Knox Press, 1960, 2 vols).
2   F. F. Bruce, *Jesus: Past, Present and Future* (Eastbourne: Kingsway, 1998), 77–78.
3   Thomas, *Principles of Theology*, 82.
4   Donne, *Christ Ascended*, 37.

Christ's intercession in heaven is made effective for us by the work of the Holy Spirit who is the advocate with us. In John's writings, Jesus is called an advocate with the Father (1 John 2:1), with the Holy Spirit as the advocate with us (John 14:16, 26; 15:26; 16:7). In Romans, Paul calls attention to the truth that 'Christ Jesus who died – more than that, who was raised to life – is at the right hand of God and is also interceding for us' (Rom 8:34). Notice that although Paul mentions the resurrection of Jesus, he also implies the ascension of Jesus. (In a similar way, in Revelation 1:18 Jesus describes himself as 'the Living One; I was dead, and now look, I am alive for ever and ever!' The ascension is implied because in Revelation Jesus is in heaven.)

Christ the ascended priest is interceding for us. F F Bruce writes that Rom 8:33–34 means that: 'Christ, raised by God to the highest place that heaven affords, is his people's counsel for the defence, not their prosecutor.'[5] He continues:

> It is remarkable in how many interchangeable ways Paul speaks of the present work of Christ and the work of the Spirit. If Christ intercedes for us, so does the Spirit; the freedom for which Christ has set us free is the freedom of the Spirit; we are 'in Christ' and 'in the Spirit'; Christ is in us and so is the Spirit. The present work of Christ, then, so far as Paul's account is concerned cannot be dissociated from the present work of the Spirit.[6]

---

5   Bruce, *Jesus: Past, Present and Future*, 68.
6   Bruce, *Jesus: Past, Present and Future*, 69.

The ascended Jesus as our representative and pledge

Christ's presence in heaven as glorified and ascended human being is the pledge of our own place before God in eternity. Christ who took flesh at the incarnation did not discard the flesh when he ascended into heaven. Gerrit Scott Dawson comments:

> The Godhead is not stripped of humanity, but adorned with it. The incarnation was not a lightning strike that is brilliant one moment but gone the next. No – though he is in heaven, he remains one of us, wearing the clothes of flesh he acquired on earth, even to eternity.[7]

He bore his flesh, fully human and now glorified, into the sanctuary of heaven itself because he acts as both representative and pledge. Dawson mentions a sermon on the ascension by Maximus of Turin (died 475 AD):

> The heart of the miracle is not just that the Son of God returned to whence he came, but that in doing so 'He brought to the Father the manhood which He had assumed from the earth'. ... As he ascends, creation is healed. The gulf between heaven and earth caused by human sin is bridged ... The 'flesh of man' is able to go where it was always intended but had ever been prevented since

---

7   Gerrit Scott Dawson, *Jesus Ascended: The Meaning of Christ's Continuing Incarnation* (London: T&T Clark International, 2004), 43.

> the Fall – into the courts of heaven and the immediate presence of God. This is the foretaste of 'the glorious freedom of the children of God' in which the entire creation will be 'liberated from its bondage to decay' (Romans 8:21). The ascending, triumphant King is the firstfruit of the new creation. Such is the victory procession of the ascension![8]

Under the Levitical priesthood, the high priests would wear a breastplate or ephod, on which were set precious stones bearing the names of the twelve tribes of Israel. Acting as their representative, the priest would literally have his people on his heart as he bore the offering for them. Christ came as the high priest not for Israel alone but for all of humanity. He bore our names not engraved on an external ephod but written in the flesh of his human nature. His priestly work in heaven and on earth must be done as a human for humans: 'For this reason he had to be made like them, fully human in every way, in order that he might become a merciful and faithful high priest in service to God, and that he might make atonement for the sins of the people' (Heb 2:17).

Jesus' presence in heaven as a glorified man is the pledge of our own future presence in heaven as glorified men and women. His presence at the right hand gives us a clear hope 'as an anchor for the soul, firm and secure. It enters the inner sanctuary behind the curtain, where our forerunner, Jesus, has entered on our behalf. He has become a high priest forever,

---

[8] Dawson, *Jesus Ascended*, 70–71.

in the order of Melchizedek' (Heb 6:19–20). In John's Gospel, Jesus had promised his disciples that he would go as a forerunner when he said he would go to prepare a place for them (John 14:2). Dawson writes:

> The ascension inaugurates a double pledge of our future in the person of Jesus. The first, we recognise easily as the deposit in our flesh of the Holy Spirit, who was received from the Father by the ascended Son and then poured out on his disciples (Acts 2:3-4). But Tertullian discerns that as Jesus went up still wearing our flesh, he now holds in himself the pledge of the resurrection bodies and eternal life in which we will partake.
>
> The person of Jesus is our hope. Redeeming and transforming our nature, he has taken it to heaven where he bears it now faithfully before his Father, in our name and on our behalf ... Jesus ascended is himself the promise and the hope that we will share in that glory, now in part but one day in full.[9]

Paul and other writers: seated with Christ in heaven

Beyond Hebrews, the other New Testament letters not only show Christ to be ascended but invite us to find our identity in him, and in heaven.

---

9   Dawson, *Jesus Ascended*, 88, 90.

For Paul as for Hebrews, the resurrection and ascension of Christ form part of a single overall movement with two distinct parts: 'Since, then, you have been raised with Christ, set your hearts on things above, where Christ is, seated at the right hand of God. Set your minds on things above, not on earthly things' (Col 3:1–2). Christ who was raised is now seated in heaven (verse 1, also Eph 1:20). He is interceding for us from the right hand (Rom 8:34, see also the previous section), the position to which he was exalted after the humiliation of the cross (Phil 2:8). We await his return as the Saviour from heaven, who will transform our bodies to be like his body (Phil 3:20–21).

Peter's first letter also connects the resurrection and ascension of Christ, 'who has gone into heaven and is at God's right hand – with angels, authorities and powers in submission to him' (1 Pet 3:22).

Paul develops the theme of Christ's supremacy over spiritual powers in the teaching of Ephesians and Colossians that Christian believers are seated with Christ.

Seated with Christ (Ephesians and Colossians)

According to Ephesians 1:21, Christ is seated at the right hand of God, 'far above all rule and authority, power and dominion, and every name that is invoked, not only in the present age but also in the one to come.' Because Ephesus was a centre for magic (see Acts 19:19), the spiritual powers would likely have held lingering power over Christian believers who needed to be reminded that their Lord dwells far above those powers. Someone who believes in Christ is 'included' in him (Eph 1:13) with the result that where Christ is, those who are in Christ are also.

For the fearful Christian, this means that we too are seated with Christ: 'And God raised us up with Christ and seated us with him in the heavenly realms in Christ Jesus' (Eph 2:6). Colossians 3:3 picks up the same thought: 'For you died, and your life is now hidden with Christ in God'. Our being raised with Christ (Col 3:1) is synonymous with our being seated with Christ (Eph 2:6).

Whereas Hebrews and John envision two advocates, Christ with the Father and the Spirit with us, Paul describes a single locus 'in Christ'. Because Christ is seated at the right hand of God, we too participate in his ascension. In both cases of course, we receive through the Spirit the benefits achieved for us by Christ through the cross, resurrection *and ascension into heaven.*

The immediate benefit for Paul is that we share in the victory that Christ has achieved over his enemies. He is seated 'far above all rule and authority, power and dominion, and every name that is invoked, not only in the present age but also in the one to come' (Eph 1:21). And just as we have been seated with Christ according to Ephesians, we have been raised with Christ according to Colossians, where Paul tells us that Christ disarmed the powers and authorities and made a public spectacle of them, triumphing over them by the cross (Col 2:15). We share in this victory by union with Christ through the Holy Spirit.

Because we are included in Christ who is seated at the right hand, the focus of our attention must be on heaven rather than on earth. Paul's application of

Christ's victory begins with an exhortation to 'set your hearts on things above, where Christ is, seated at the right hand of God. Set your minds on things above, not on earthly things' (Col 3:1–2). We will see below that Christian worship also lifts our hearts to Christ rather than bringing Christ down to earth.

The ascension implied (Romans and Corinthians)

It is notable that Paul's major letters say so little about the ascension of Christ. The resurrection is treated at length in 1 Corinthians 15, the atonement in Romans 1–3, union with Christ in Romans 5–8, and the ministry of the Spirit in Romans 8. Where does Paul mention the ascension?

It is true that the ascension is assumed rather than explicit here. The sacrifice of Christ implies a priest, which Hebrews expounds; the life of the Spirit implies the exaltation of the Christ who sends the Spirit; the Spirit brings Christ's presence because Christ himself is bodily absent from earth. Romans 10:6–7 mentions that Christ came down from heaven and came up from the dead: 'But the righteousness that is by faith says: "Do not say in your heart, 'Who will ascend into heaven?'" (that is, to bring Christ down) "or 'Who will descend into the deep?'" (that is, to bring Christ up from the dead).' But that is hardly a clear statement of the doctrine of the ascension.

The clearest explanation seems to be that the resurrection and ascension of Paul are distinct but so strongly connected that to state one implies the other. In his chapter about the resurrection (1 Cor 15), Paul affirms that Christ has been raised from the dead and that as he is the 'firstfruits of those who have fallen asleep' (1 Cor 15:20), others will also be raised when Christ returns (verse 23). But this is not all:

> Then the end will come, when he hands over the kingdom to God the Father after he has destroyed all dominion, authority and power. For he must reign until he has put all his enemies under his feet. (1 Cor 15:24–25)

The implication of the resurrection of Christ from the dead is that he reigns *now,* but that 'all dominion, authority and power' are still to be done away with. We wait to see the ascended king, Jesus, revealed at his return. The pledge that he will return is his resurrection and implied in that resurrection is the ascension.

The giver of gifts (Ephesians 4)

The ascended Christ is also the head of the church, to whom he distributes the gifts of his ascension. Psalm 68, quoted in Ephesians 4:8, speaks of a victorious king's accession (as do Psa 24 and 47). This is the king who 'descended to the lower, earthly regions' (Eph 4:9) and 'ascended higher than all the heavens, in order to fill the whole universe' (Eph 4:10). The descent could refer only to the incarnation, or it could refer to his incarnation and then descent to the realm of the dead. The ascent clearly refers to his ascension to the right hand of God, above all other spiritual places.

Christ ascends as a victorious king who then distributes coronation gifts to his people. These gifts are spiritual gifts to equip the church for the work of ministry (Eph 4:11–13) and to bring the body to maturity (Eph 4:14–16). It is striking that this brings us back to the day of Pentecost where the gift of the Spirit was the visible manifestation of the unseen coronation in heaven. The Spirit's presence and gifts in the church are both the evidence and the consequence of Jesus' enthronement in heaven.

The Lamb that was slain (Revelation)

The vision given to John is of Jesus 'who is, and who was, and who is to come' and who says 'I am the Living One; I was dead, and now look, I am alive for ever and ever!' (Rev 1:4, 18). John, it seems, is given a vision of the *risen* Lord Jesus. In light of what we have seen above it seems to me better to say that the vision is of the risen *and ascended* Lord: he is the King of kings (Rev 1:5, 17:14, 19:16). The book of Revelation opens a window onto a world where Christ is "uniquely King *of* the church and irresistibly King *over* the world."[10]

It is notable that at no point is Calvary, nor indeed the incarnation which it requires, left behind in Christ's ascension: he is the 'Lamb, looking as if it had been slain' (Rev 5:6, 12; 13:8) displaying the marks of his sacrifice. The vision in Revelation, which depicts Christ's rule from heaven through his sacrifice, overlaps with the image in the letter to the Hebrews, where Christ offers of his sacrifice of himself in 'heaven itself' (Heb 9:24).

The rule of Christ from heaven breaks through into this world through the witness, work and prayer of the church on earth. Pastor Peter Lewis comments:

> And above all, it is the prayer life
> and preaching of the church which

---

10 Peter Lewis, *The Glory of Christ* (Carlisle: Paternoster, 1992), 391, emphasis original.

invades Satan's territory, defeating 'principalities and powers', bringing the light and life of the gospel to societies in spiritual darkness, effectively calling men and women to Christ, the once-crucified, and now-reigning Lord. It is by such means, as well as in unseen and independent ways, that Christ Jesus exercises his rule, extends his kingdom and fulfils God's eternal purposes.[11]

Conclusion and summary

We can summarise our survey of the New Testament references to the ascension of Christ in the following propositions.

1. The New Testament has much more to say about the ascension of Christ than just the narrative passages of Luke 24:51 and Acts 1:9. The ascension is mentioned by every major section of the New Testament. It is not a minor doctrine.

2. The ascension marks Jesus' departure from earth and return to heaven. It is neither a retirement from ministry nor a return to the way things were before the incarnation. The ascension is a shift in the base of Jesus' ministry from earth to heaven.

3. Jesus ascends to heaven to be installed as king, victorious over his enemies and generous with gifts to his people. He receives all authority in heaven and earth, fulfilling the vision of Daniel

---

[11] Lewis, *Glory of Christ*, 392.

7:13–14. He empowers his people to announce that rule through evangelism and he distributes gifts, namely the Holy Spirit.

4. The ascension is and should be a cause of great joy for the disciples, even though it requires Jesus' bodily absence from them on earth.

5. Jesus' ascension is his return to the Father. As a result of his return, Jesus and the Father send the Advocate, the Holy Spirit. We now have an advocate with the Father (Jesus) and an advocate with us (the Spirit).

6. Because of Jesus' ascension and consequent authority and gift of the Holy Spirit, Jesus' followers will now do greater things than had been the case during Jesus' earthly ministry. This too is a source of joy.

7. The book of Acts describes the earthly outworking of Jesus' heavenly ministry. He did not hand his ministry over to the Spirit or the church: Acts tells of what he continued to do and teach after his ascension through the church empowered by the Spirit.

8. Jesus' ascension as high priest completes his work of atonement by offering his sacrifice of himself in the true tabernacle, heaven itself. His going into 'the Most Holy Place once for all' (Heb 9:12) fulfils the shadows that were the Old Testament priesthood. Because he has gone through the heavens in his ascension, we have confidence with God for he remains to intercede for us for ever.

9. Jesus ascended with his human nature. His presence in heaven as glorified man is the pledge of our resurrection, glorification and presence with God in the new creation.

10. Finally, through union with Christ we are seated with Christ in heaven. We can share in his victory, and raise our hearts to heaven, where he is.

How then is this doctrine reflected in the life and worship of the church?

4. Anglican Witnesses to the Ascension

How does the Biblical witness to the ascension of Christ shape the life and belief of the Church of England, according to its formularies – the Articles of Religion, the *Book of Common Prayer* and the *Ordinal*?

The Articles

The Thirty-Nine Articles of Religion were born of the Reformation and while they do not completely amount to a Confession of Faith, they summarise the doctrine of the Church of England as we have received it: 'the Articles were not intended to supersede but to supplement the old credal statements with carefully reasoned explanations of their meaning and implications.'[12]

Article 4: Of the resurrection of Christ

The fourth Article includes the Ascension of Christ:

---

12 Charles Neil and J. M. Willoughby, *The Tutorial Prayer Book: For the Teacher, the Student, and the General Reader* (London: The Harrison Trust, 1912), 539. For accessible introductions to the Articles see Gerald L. Bray, *The Faith We Confess: An Exposition of the Thirty-Nine Articles* (London: Latimer Trust, 2009); John H. Rodgers, *Knowing Anglicanism – the Faith of Anglicans* (Newport Beach: Anglican House, 2021). The Articles are not a Confession because Anglican belief is declared in the church's practice of worship. That is why the Church's Formularies consist of the Articles and two liturgical texts, the *Book of Common Prayer* and the *Ordinal*. See Martin Davie, *Lex Orandi, Lex Credendi: Liturgy, Doctrine and Scripture in History and Today* (London: Latimer Trust, 2019).

IV Of the Resurrection of Christ
Christ did truly rise again from death, and took again his body, with flesh, bones, and all things appertaining to the perfection of Man's nature; wherewith he ascended into Heaven, and there sitteth, until he return to judge all Men at the last day.

We notice immediately that the Ascension is obscured by the Resurrection: surely the Article could have been named the Resurrection *and Ascension* of Christ because 'following Scripture, the Article makes no distinction between the Resurrection and the Ascension as actual facts'.[1]

According to the Article, Christ's resurrection was bodily, with flesh and bones. And yet this body was different to ours because it held 'all things appertaining to the perfection of Man's nature'. Griffith Thomas comments: 'Thus, the true description of the Resurrection seems to be that it was an objective reality, and yet not merely physical resuscitation. It was the same, yet different; different, yet the same'.[2]

Christ's ascension too was with this same body, 'wherewith he ascended'. As we saw above, Christ did not shed his human nature at the ascension but took it with him into heaven. Griffith Thomas notes that the Docetism of the early Gnostics had been revived in the sixteenth century.[3] Docetism was the view that the body of Christ was not real but only seeming human, and so, 'either the sufferings were only apparent, or

---

1 Thomas, *Principles of Theology*, 74.
2 Thomas, *Principles of Theology*, 74.
3 Thomas, *Principles of Theology*, 73.

else the redeemer who could not suffer was separate from the man in whom he appeared'.[4] However, the Bible's teaching is that Jesus was made flesh in every way as we are (as we saw in Hebrews above). The Article reinforces the bodily resurrection of Jesus and the bodily ascension of Jesus.

Articles 28–31: The Lord's Supper

One great controversy of the time of composing the Articles was in what sense Jesus' body is present in the elements of Holy Communion. The answer depends on how we understand Jesus to be absent from earth through his ascension into heaven. As we saw earlier, John records Jesus telling his disciples about 'going away' because his ascension would mean that he was bodily absent. At the same time, he spoke of the Advocate whom the Father would send in Jesus' name. The question is not new:

> The problem of the presence and the absence, of the Lord who is seen but not seen, who is at table but not at table, who is both with us and away from us, who is walked with yet awaited, has dogged ecclesiology from the beginning.[5]

According to the Reformed view, the eternal Son of God became human at the incarnation. He is united to the flesh but he is not confined to the location of his

---

4 Sinclair B. Ferguson, J. I. Packer, and David F. Wright, *New Dictionary of Theology* (Leicester: Inter-Varsity Press, 1988), 201.
5 Farrow, *Ascension and Ecclesia*, 8.

body.[6] Thus Christ can be present everywhere as God and only locally as man.

The Heidelberg Catechism (1563) expresses Calvin's teaching in questions 46 to 48:

> 46. Q. What do you confess when you say, He ascended into heaven?
> A. That Christ, before the eyes of His disciples, was taken up from the earth into heaven, and that He is there for our benefit until He comes again to judge the living and the dead.
>
> 47. Q. Is Christ, then, not with us until the end of the world, as He has promised us?
> A. Christ is true man and true God. With respect to His human nature He is no longer on earth, but with respect to His divinity, majesty, grace, and Spirit He is never absent from us.
>
> 48. Q. But are the two natures in Christ not separated from each other if His human nature is not present wherever His divinity is?
> A. Not at all, for His divinity has no limits and is present everywhere. So it must follow that His divinity is indeed beyond the human nature which He has taken on and nevertheless is within this human

---

6 Calvin, *Institutes*, 2.13.4.

nature and remains personally united with it.

For Calvin, the human and divine attributes of Christ are not communicable. Sometimes Scripture describes attributes that can only belong to Christ's human nature, such as growing (Luke 2:52). They are applied to Christ because he is truly human. Other attributes refer to his divinity, such as the statement that 'before Abraham was born, I am!' (John 8:58). They are applied to Christ because he is truly God. Yet another statement such as 'the church of God, which he bought with his own blood' (Acts 20:28) communicates characteristics of both Christ's human and divine natures. For Calvin, statements that embrace both natures connect the two natures but do not imply any 'confusion of substance'.[7]

By contrast Lutherans hold that there is an exchange of the divine and human attributes in Christ – especially a sharing by the human nature of the divine attribute of omnipresence.[8] This affects their understanding of the Lord's Supper because Christ's body shares the divine characteristic of omnipresence and becomes ubiquitous. In this way. Christ's body *can* be present in and under the bread on earth, whereas in Calvin's understanding, it cannot be present in this way because Christ's body in heaven must be local as it was on earth: 'Christ imparted immortality to his own flesh but did not remove its nature from it.'[9]

Calvin's view – in contrast to the Lutherans' – is that we

---

7   Calvin, *Institutes,* 2.14.23 and David B. Calhoun, *Knowing God and Ourselves: Reading Calvin's Institutes Devotionally* (Edinburgh: Banner of Truth, 2016), 126–27.
8   Calhoun, *Knowing God and Ourselves*, 126.
9   Calvin, *Institutes,* 4.17.28.

partake of Christ's body not by bringing his body down to earth but by lifting our hearts to heaven:

> But if we are lifted up to heaven with our eyes and minds, to seek Christ there, in the glory of his Kingdom, as the symbols invite us to him in his wholeness, so under the symbol of bread, we shall be fed by his body, under the symbol of wine, we shall separately drink his blood, to enjoy him at last in his wholeness. For, though he has taken his flesh away from us, and in his body has ascended into heaven, yet he sits at the right hand of the Father – that is, he reigns in the Father's power, and majesty and glory.[10]

With this background we can see why Article 28 on the Lord's Supper declares that 'The Body of Christ is given, taken, and eaten, in the Supper, only after an heavenly and spiritual manner. And the mean whereby the Body of Christ is received and eaten in the Supper is Faith.' It follows that the Sacrament of the Lord's Supper is not to be reserved, carried about, lifted up or worshipped.

According to the Articles, Christ is absent from earth as man because he is in heaven, but present everywhere in heaven and on earth as God. His presence in heaven as a man pledges and guarantees the redemption of our bodies and our future place with God.

---

10   Calvin, *Institutes*, 4.17.18.

The Creeds and the Litany

The early church made the ascension central to their faith and included it in every summary of faith, from the Apostles' Creed (AD 120–150) through to the Reformation Confessions.[11]

The three creeds accepted by the Church of England 'to be received and believed: for they may be proved by most certain warrants of holy Scripture' are the Nicene, Athanasian and Apostles' Creeds.[12] All three creeds mention the ascension of Christ who: 'ascended into heaven and sitteth on the right hand of the Father' (Nicene Creed), 'Ascended into heaven, and sitteth of the right hand of God the Father Almighty' (Apostles' Creed), and 'ascended into heaven, sitteth on the right hand of the Father, God Almighty'(Athanasian Creed).[13]

The Litany or General Supplication in the *Book of Common Prayer* calls for deliverance because of the ministry of Christ which includes the Ascension:

> By the mystery of thy holy Incarnation; by thy holy Nativity and Circumcision; by thy Baptism, Fasting, and Temptation, *Good Lord, deliver us.*
>
> By thine Agony and bloody Sweat; by thy Cross and Passion; by thy precious Death and Burial; by thy glorious Resurrection and

---

11 Schreiner, *Ascension of Christ*, 14.
12 Article 8 'Of The Three Creeds'.
13 A useful introduction to the Athanasian Creed is Martin Davie, *The Athanasian Creed* (London: Latimer Trust, 2019). See also companions to the *Book of Common Prayer*.

> Ascension; and by the coming of the Holy Ghost, *Good Lord, deliver us.*

While the Creeds and Litany do not place undue emphasis on the ascension of Christ, their regular use in corporate as well as private worship reinforces the place of the ascension as a main doctrine.

The Collects

Ascension is marked forty days after Easter and ten days before Pentecost (also known as Whit Sunday). Since Ascension Day always falls on a Thursday, Ascensiontide includes a collect for Ascension Day and another for the Sunday following.

Ascension Day

> **Ascension Day**
> GRANT, we beseech thee, Almighty God, that like as we do believe thy only-begotten Son our Lord Jesus Christ to have ascended into the heavens; so we may also in heart and mind thither ascend, and with him continually dwell, who liveth and reigneth with thee and the Holy Ghost, one God, world without end. Amen.

Some consider that Cranmer's view of the Lord's Supper is hard to pin down because his liturgical texts point in one direction while his writings on the subject point in a different direction: was he Catholic or Protestant on the issue? For Ashely Null, the Collect for Ascension Day helps answer these questions:

> For Cranmer, the miracle of Holy Communion is not that Christ's body comes down to us from Heaven, but that we ascend, as the collect says, in heart and mind, to where Christ's physical body is now present – the right hand of God. The Holy Spirit draws us to Christ's real presence in Heaven, and there he truly feeds us with his true flesh and blood.[14]

The Collect reinforces the teaching of the Article that Christ's body is in heaven and encourages us to ascend to him rather than seek to bring him down to us. The ascension of Christ shapes our worship and the Collect prays that we might 'continually dwell' with Christ in heaven.

Sunday after Ascension Day

> **Sunday after Ascension Day**
> O GOD the King of glory, who hast exalted thine only Son Jesus Christ with great triumph unto thy kingdom in heaven: We beseech thee, leave us not comfortless; but send to us thine Holy Ghost to comfort us, and exalt us unto the same place whither our Saviour Christ is gone before, who liveth and reigneth with thee and the Holy Ghost, one God, world without end. Amen.

---

[14] Ashley Null, *Knowing Anglicanism – Eastertide: Meditations on the Easter Collects of Thomas Cranmer* (Newport Beach: Anglican House, 2024), 103.

The Collect opens by declaring Christ to have been exalted with great triumph, reflecting one of the themes of the ascension (see especially the Synoptic Gospels). The request to 'leave us not comfortless' is at first glance rather a strange one: surely since that first Day of Pentecost the Spirit has been poured out on the church and he does not need to be poured out again? The Collect has not forgotten about Pentecost, nor is it seeking to re-enact the waiting period endured by the disciples in Jerusalem. The emphasis is rather on the *comfort* that the Spirit brings which contrasts with the pre-Reformation view of the Spirit's ministry as one of shame and self-condemnation. Cranmer put this truth into practice by including in his order for the Lord's Supper four verses known to us as the Comfortable Words (Matt 11:28, John 3:16, 1 Tim 1:15, 1 John 2:1).[15]

Second, the Collect prays that God may 'exalt us unto the same place whither our Saviour Christ is gone before'. This becomes possible through the comfort that Christ brings through his Spirit. Ashley Null notes:

> Scripture clearly teaches us that Jesus is our true comfort, now and forever. That's why Cranmer put these four verses at the very heart of the Communion service, immediately before the minister says, 'Lift up your hearts.' For when our hearts have been comforted and strengthened by Jesus' loving actions for us and in us, only then do we find the power and confidence

---

15 Null, *Eastertide*, 112–14.

to raise our hearts and minds to his presence at the right hand of God.[16]

The endings of Collects

Eighteen Collects in the *Book of Common Prayer* finish with a trinitarian ending, such as 'through him who liveth and reigneth with thee and the Holy Ghost, now and ever. Amen.' Every time a Collect is prayed with such an ending, we are reminded of the reign of the ascended Christ. The Collects that end in this way are those for the first Sunday in Advent, the third Sunday in Advent, Christmas Day, the Sunday after Christmas Day, the sixth Sunday after Epiphany, the seventh Sunday after Epiphany, the first Sunday in Lent, the first and third Collects for Good Friday, Easter Day, Monday in Easter Week, Tuesday in Easter Week, Ascension Day, the Sunday after Ascension Day, Whit Sunday, Monday in Whitsun Week, Tuesday in Whitsun Week and St Matthew the Apostle (21 September). Also the first Collect for the Sovereign in the Order for Holy Communion.

The Collects for the fourth Sunday in Advent and for St Thomas the Apostle (21 December) end with 'thy Son our Lord, to whom with thee and the Holy Ghost be honour and glory, world without end. Amen,' which alludes to the exaltation of Christ now in heaven. The phrase 'world without end' is confusing given our belief in the return of Christ and subsequent new creation. If the 'world' here refers to the situation that honour are due to the Father, Son and Holy Spirit, then that is a situation that is without end.

---

16 Null, *Eastertide*, 126.

The Collect for St Stephen's Day (26 December) ends with a reference to the martyr's vision of the exalted Son of Man (Acts 7:55–56):

> GRANT, O Lord, that in all our sufferings here upon earth, for the testimony of thy truth, we may stedfastly look up to heaven, and by faith behold the glory that shall be revealed; and, being filled with the Holy Ghost, may learn to love and bless our persecutors by the example of thy first Martyr Saint Stephen, who prayed for his murderers to thee, *O blessed Jesus, who standest at the right hand of God to succour all those that suffer for thee, our only Mediator and Advocate.* Amen.[17]

When the Collects are used regularly, they remind us of the truth and significance of the ascension.

The service of Holy Communion

The focus of this service is of course on the saving death of Jesus rather than his resurrection or ascension. Nevertheless:

- The last of the Comfortable Words is 1 John 2:1, 'If any man sin, we have an Advocate with the Father, Jesus Christ the righteous; and he is the propitiation for our sins.' Jesus is the

---

[17] Emphasis added. 'Standest' here must have the sense of 'remains' rather than 'is not seated'. The sense appears also in the line 'I know that while in heav'n He stands/no tongue can bid me thence depart' from Charitie L. Bancroft's hymn *Before the Throne of God Above*.

Advocate *with the Father* through his ascension.

- The Proper Preface for Ascension Day says: 'through thy most dearly beloved Son Jesus Christ our Lord; who after his most glorious Resurrection manifestly appeared to all his Apostles, and *in their sight ascended up into heaven to prepare a place for us; that where he is, thither we might also ascend, and reign with him in glory.*'

- The first prayer after Communion asks that 'we and all thy whole Church may obtain remission of our sins, and *all other benefits of his passion*'. These 'other benefits' are the fruits of Christ's passion (suffering) which are offered by his ascension through the heavens into the true temple. Through Christ's priestly offering, those benefits become available to us.

- The Gloria that follows praises the Son 'that sittest at the right hand of God the Father'.

- The final rubric about kneeling to receive Communion makes clear that this is for good order and not because the bread or wine are being worshipped:

> It is here declared that thereby no Adoration is intended, or ought to be done, either unto the Sacramental Bread or Wine there bodily received, or unto any Corporal Presence of Christ's natural Flesh and Blood. For the Sacramental Bread and Wine remain still in their very natural

> substances, and therefore may not be adored; (for that were Idolatry, to be abhorred of all faithful Christians;) and the natural Body and Blood of our Saviour Christ are in Heaven, and not here; it being against the truth of Christ's natural Body to be at one time in more places than one.

The rubric is a clear reminder of a Reformed rather than Lutheran understanding of Christ's divine and human natures. It is known as the 'black' rubric because it was added to the *Book of Common Prayer* after the other rubrics had already been printed in red.

Morning and Evening Prayer

The introduction to confession ends with 'Wherefore I pray and beseech you, as many as are here present, to accompany me with a pure heart and humble voice unto the throne of the heavenly grace, saying after me...' This is a reference to Hebrews and our access to the throne of grace because of and through our great high priest.

Among the closing prayers, the one for clergy and people ends 'for the honour of our Advocate and mediator, Jesus Christ'.

Conclusion

The Anglican Formularies bear witness to the doctrine, feast and reality of the ascension of Christ. The doctrine of his bodily ascent into heaven, summarised in Article 4, indicates that Christ's presence in the Lord's Supper is spiritual and rejects the Lutheran teaching that Christ's body is ubiquitous. The feast of the ascension is marked by Collects for the day itself (always a Thursday) and the Sunday following but there is no separate liturgy for the service itself. Anglican worship, whether or not it includes the Lord's Supper, is oriented to lifting our hearts to the Lord who is in heaven and not to bringing him down to us on earth. The other reality of the ascension is that he who ascended into heaven will one day return: Anglican worship prepares us to 'wait for his Son from heaven, whom he raised from the dead – Jesus, who rescues us from the coming wrath' (1 Thess 1:9–10).

5. Doctrinal and Pastoral Connections

The ascension brings us to the heart of the gospel for without it the benefits won by Christ can neither be brought to God or made available to us. Once we see this, the ascension helps us to make sense of the whole narrative of Jesus' descent from and return to heaven. Like every other doctrine, the ascension must do more than make sense of the biblical narrative; it must open the door to the Christian life and lead us forward. This section aims to draw together the threads of what has been said above and point out avenues for application to life and doctrine so that we may better obey Paul's command to set our hearts and minds on things above, where Christ is seated at the right hand of God (Col 3:1, 3).

a) Doctrinal connections

We will consider briefly the doctrinal implications of the ascension for our understanding of the Trinity, Christology, the incarnation, anthropology and cosmology.

The Trinity

The three Persons of Father, Son and Holy Spirit are as indivisibly joined in the ascension of Christ as they are in everything else. The Father sent the Son and in his ascension, Jesus would return to the Father (John 20:17). The Son was not separated from the Father during Jesus' earthly ministry and because of the work of the Holy Spirit (John 14:18) neither is the ascended Jesus separated from his church. Jesus now crowned with glory rules from heaven and is with his church on earth by the Holy Spirit. At no point in the incarnation and ascension of Christ are the persons of the Trinity divided from one another.

Christology and incarnation

At the incarnation, the Second person of the Trinity became flesh and made his dwelling among us (John 1:14). Jesus is one person whose human and divine natures are inseparably united. The union continues even now in heaven, as we saw earlier. Dawson comments:

> The Godhead is not stripped of humanity, but adorned with it. The incarnation was not a lightning strike that is brilliant one moment but gone the next. No – though he is in heaven, he remains one of us, wearing the clothes of flesh he acquired on earth, even to eternity.[1]

A right understanding of the ascension of Christ protects us from Christological errors. Dawson again:

> The doctrine of the ascension keeps us from collapsing our understanding of the person of Christ into any of the Christological distortions of the present age. For not only does Jesus continue now in our flesh, he continues in his divinity. The fully human Jesus is and ever shall be fully God. The Son of God from eternity, in the fullness of time, took our humanity

---

1 Dawson, *Jesus Ascended*, 43.

> up into himself as he became incarnate in Jesus. Now, he will keep our humanity in himself beyond all time.[2]

Jesus' ascension into heaven as a man also informs our understanding of how he is present on earth now. As we saw above in the discussion of the Articles of Religion and the Black Rubric in the Service of Holy Communion according to the *Book of Common Prayer*, the Anglican Reformers' view is that Christ is bodily present in heaven because of the ascension and spiritually present everywhere on earth through the ministry of the Holy Spirit. These follow because Jesus remains incarnate: the ascension does not reverse or undo the incarnation but affirms it.

Anthropology

Jesus' ascension into heaven as a man is the pledge of our own presence in heaven *with our human natures* which will be raised and glorified to be like his body (Phil 3:21). 'Christ descended in order to bring God to humanity, and he ascended to bring humanity to God.'[3] Jesus' presence at the right hand of the Father gives us a clear hope (Heb 6:19–20). Peter Lewis comments:

> In Christ deity and humanity, uncreated God and created man, yes, even Spirit and flesh, are everlastingly joined. There is a man in heaven, who is also God: eternally beloved, infinitely valued. He now

---

2 Dawson, *Jesus Ascended*, 91.
3 Schreiner, *Ascension of Christ*, 105.

> gives massive significance to us as human beings and to every part of our humanness.[4]

Oliver O'Donovan makes an interesting comment on the difference between the resurrection and the ascension. The resurrection has a double aspect: it looks backward to vindicate Christ who died and it looks forward to the glorification of Christ in heaven.

> When the resurrection is distinguished from the ascension (as it is by Saint Luke and indirectly by Saint John – cf. 20:17) it looks backwards. ... When, however, the resurrection is presented alone without the ascension (as it is by Saint Mark and Saint Matthew) it looks forwards. Already Christ is transformed; the physical has been assumed by the spiritual, the man of dust by the heavenly man. The resurrection appearances are encounters with divine power and authority. Humanity is elevated to that which it has never enjoyed before, the seat at God's right hand which belongs to his Son.[5]

Both Jesus' incarnation and his ascension affirm the material world. In contrast to the Gnostic view that salvation was an escape from the material world and

---

4 Lewis, *Glory of Christ*, 379.
5 O'Donovan, *Resurrection and Moral Order*, 57. See also above on Hebrews under 'Jesus our Representative and Pledge'.

from the physical human body, the gospel of Christ redeems and transforms the body through the atoning death, powerful resurrection and glorious ascension of Jesus Christ. Against Docetic ideas that Christ only 'seemed' human, the ascension affirms that Christ is fully human and therefore that Christian believers shall be fully redeemed.

Cosmology

When Jesus ascended he clearly left the earth, but *where* did he go? The answer depends on our understanding of the nature of the heavens and the earth, that is cosmology. The three options for where Jesus is now are *nowhere* (spiritualising the ascension), *somewhere* (whether within space–time or outside it) or *everywhere* (so that he is ubiquitous, as the Lutherans hold).

Nowhere?

Origen (185–254 AD) was an early advocate of spiritualising the ascension. While Origen affirmed the incarnation of Jesus, Christ was 'the human embodiment of the one soul that did not fall away, a soul eternally united to the divine Logos, a soul who descended freely in pursuit of the fallen in order to show them the way back home. But because only the mind can participate in the Logos, Christ's ascension is of the mind only.'[6] Origen anticipated Friedrich Schleiermacher (1768–1834) and Georg Hegel (1770–1831) who also spiritualised the ascension in the mistaken attempt to recover the human Jesus. This turns out to be Docetism (in other words, that Jesus only seemed human) by another name:

---

6   Farrow, *Ascension Theology*, 20.

> Modern theology in its Origenist mode has compromised all its attempts at such a recovery [sc. of the human Jesus], however helpful some of them may be, for the simple reason that it has no room for the risen, ascended and coming one as a man; that is, as a particular human being. Eschatological Docetism – looking only for the divine in Jesus by way of his effects on the church or on the race as a whole – is still Docetism after all.[7]

A spiritualised ascension denies the full humanity of Christ *and* our own humanity: 'Simply put, our choice is between a doctrine of the ascension that truly affirms our humanity in Christ and one that secretly or openly denies it.'[8] Origen was condemned as a heretic and Schleiermacher celebrated as a father of modern liberal theology; neither are right about the ascension. If Jesus truly came from earth and took flesh then he truly returned to heaven: but where is that?

Somewhere?

When Jesus ascended he went to heaven, the place where God is. What kind of 'place' is it?

Wayne Grudem proposes that the heaven to which Jesus has ascended is 'clearly a localization of heaven in the space–time universe' and that 'the ascension of Jesus into heaven is designed to teach us that heaven

---

7 Farrow, *Ascension Theology*, 29.
8 Farrow, *Ascension Theology*, xii.

does exist as a place in the space–time universe.'[9] Dawson robustly disagrees:

> But never did Christians believe Jesus had gone to a 'place' we could locate if only we had the right visual equipment. Calvin quips, 'What? Do we place Christ midway among the spheres? Or do we build a cottage for him among the planets? Heaven we regard as the magnificent palace of God outstripping all this world's fabric'.[10]

Heaven is not a place within space–time because God's dwelling is not within his creation. He is distinct from his creation. If we think about how God relates to time rather than to space, Boethius (480–524 AD) stresses that God has a fundamentally different relationship to time – we are bound by it, he is not. God is more than 'outside' of time: he has a qualitatively different relationship to time such that all past, present and future events in the created world are equally present to him.[11] In the same way, God has a qualitatively

---

9   Wayne Grudem, *Systematic Theology: An Introduction to Biblical Doctrine* (Leicester: IVP, 1994), 618.
10 Dawson, *Jesus Ascended*, 39–40, citing John Calvin, 'Second Defence of the Pious and Orthodox Faith Concerning the Sacraments' in Henry Beveridge and Jules Bonnet (eds), *Selected Works of John Calvin*, vol 2, trans. Henry Beveridge (Albany: OR: Books for the Ages, 1998), 270.
11 Gavin Ortlund, *Theological Retrieval for Evangelicals: Why We Need Our Past to Have a Future* (Wheaton: Crossway, 2019), 94. Chapter 4 (pages 89–116) is entitled 'Explorations in a Theological Metaphor: Boethius, Calvin and Torrance on the Creator/Creation Distinction'.

different relationship to space because he created it and is distinct from his creation. Heaven, the place where God is, cannot be found within time and space. Even to say that heaven is 'outside' time and space uses a spacial metaphor to describe an utter difference of kind. If Jesus ascended to heaven, then the 'place' that he ascended to is not a place within time and space. He is not in a cottage among the stars and we are not surprised that the first cosmonaut Yuri Gagarin (1934–68) did not see either God or Jesus when he peered out of his space capsule.

Jesus' ascension to heaven creates something new because he now exists somewhere that is both man's place and God's place. According to T F Torrance:

> As in the incarnation, we have to think of God the Son becoming man without ceasing to be transcendent God, so in his Ascension, we have to think of Christ as ascending above all space and time without ceasing to be man or without any diminishment of his physical, historical existence.[12]

It is not simply the translation of Christ from one realm to another but the creation of something new, the healing of time and space. It is an upgrade because heaven is now a place that is, as Gavin Ortlund expresses it, 'friendly to creaturely existence as creaturely, for instance, bodily and spatio-temporal existence.'[13] Dawson notes that the ascension, 'represents the departure of the incarnate Son of God back to the place

---

12   Thomas F. Torrance, *Atonement: The Person and Work of Christ* (Downers Grove: InterVarsity Press, 2009), 287.
13   Ortlund, *Retrieval*, 112.

where God is, taking human nature where it has never gone before.'[14] Farrow similarly says that Jesus has gone to a 'place' that is not a place in space: 'We must say that it entails the creation of a new time and place and mode of life, and that not *ex nihilo* (out of nothing) but *ex vetere* (out of the old one).[15]

Everywhere?

If Jesus is in heaven, in what sense and how is he with us now on earth? And similarly, when he was on earth, how was he in heaven? According to Calvin, Jesus in his human nature is present in one place only, just as we are in our human nature; but in his divine nature, he continued to sustain all things by his power during his earthly ministry. The teaching that the incarnate Son of God was not limited to his human flesh, but continued to uphold the univese, even while incarnate is known as the 'Extra Calvinisticum'.[16] Calvin was debating with the Lutherans on the nature of Christ's presence in the Supper. His opponents taught that aspects of the ascended Christ's human and divine nature are communicable, such that Christ in his human nature shares the quality of his divine nature to be everywhere. Because Christ's human nature is ubiquitous (everywhere), his body can be present in the bread and wine of the Lord's Supper. We saw earlier that Article 4 and the 'Black Rubric' in the service of Holy Communion according to the *Book of Common Prayer* firmly rebut the Lutheran view. According to Gavin Ortlund, 'Calvin found the Lutheran doctrine of the ubiquity of Christ "monstrous" precisely because it

---

14 Dawson, *Jesus Ascended*, 50.
15 Farrow, *Ascension Theology*, 45–46.
16 Ortlund, *Retrieval*, 100.

failed to preserve the twoness of Christ's two natures, and instead resulted in "some sort of intermediate being, which was neither God nor man."[17]

Conclusion

I find the view of Boethius, Calvin and Torrance the most persuasive, that Christ ascended to heaven, where God is, and this heaven is not bound within time and space. Torrance, Dawson and Farrow also show that the 'heaven' to which Christ ascended is changed by the ascension of man where man has not gone before.

b) Pastoral and liturgical concerns

We will consider four pastoral implications of the ascension – concerning our worship, prayer, mission and preaching.

Worship

The ascension is to be celebrated with joy, following the example of the disciples (Luke 24:52) and the teaching of Jesus that they should be glad (John 14:28). Because of Jesus' ascension we can do greater things than was possible before (John 14:12) and this too should be a cause for joy: otherwise, we repeat Mary's error of wanting to cling on to the risen Jesus (John 20:17), thus preventing him from ascending.

Jesus' sacrifice and priesthood fulfilled the types and shadows of Old Testament priesthood. He is the great high priest who offered the better sacrifice of himself and went through the curtain into the true sanctuary of heaven itself.

---

17 Ortlund, *Retrieval*, 104.

- Because these types have been fulfilled, we do not need to enact or even re-enact them in our worship. Christian worship does not make use of sacerdotal priests because Christ is the true and great high priest; Christian worship does not make sacrifice for sin because Christ is the better sacrifice offered once for all. We can, however, offer sacrifices of praise (Heb 13:15; also 1 Pet 2:9) and offer ourselves as living sacrifices (Rom 12:1–2).

- Because these types have been fulfilled by Christ, the basis of our worship is his priestly ministry, which is both a confession to hold fast (Heb 4:14, 10:23) and a confidence to exercise before God (Heb 10:19). Our worship before the Father is through Christ and with confidence because of Christ.

- Because these types have been fulfilled, the locus of our worship is no longer on earth and in tabernacles made by human hands but in heaven, where Christ is seated at the right hand of God. In our worship we lift our hearts to heaven rather than bring heaven down to us.

Lifting our hearts

Lifting our hearts to worship in this way is not natural to us and without attention we are likely to drift away, as it seems that the Hebrews (to whom the letter was written) were wont to do. We need constantly to recall the gospel and renounce the world:

> The gospel, the story of Jesus come among us, is not native to us. It is a story foreign to our sinful hearts.

> Without the discipline of a rigorous submission to the truth revealed to us, we will quickly distort the narrative and shape its meaning to be more amenable to our inclinations. Thus, we absolutely require the community of the church, the means of grace, and a consecrated leadership exercising biblical discipline to draw our attention to matters of necessity.[18]

Lifting our hearts is not a bolt-on to Christian worship: it is the basis that flows from every reminder in word and deed and song, in reading and in prayers. In this way, the practice of Christian worship truly honours the confidence that we have because Christ died, was raised and is ascended in heaven: 'In corporate worship we rise by faith to enter the heavenly assembly of the saints and angels.'[19]

We find it hard to renounce the world and set our hearts on things above because we want instant glory without the pain. According to Andrew Murray, this is foolish:

> They wonder that they have so little of the peace and joy, of the purity and power, which the Saviour gives, and which faith in Him ought

---

18 Dawson, *Jesus Ascended*, 169.
19 Edmund Clowney, 'Corporate Worship: a Means of Grace' in Philip Graham Ryken, Derek W. H. Thomas, and J. Ligon Duncan II (eds.), *Give Praise to God* (Phillipsburg, NJ, P&R, 2003), 96, cited in Tony Merida, *Gather: Loving Your Church as You Celebrate Christ Together* (Epsom, Good Book Company, 2023), 16–17.

to bring. The reason is simple, because Christ is only their Aaron, not their Melchizedek. They do indeed believe that He is ascended to heaven, and sits upon the throne of God; but they have not seen the direct connection of this with their daily spiritual life. They do not count upon Jesus working in them in the power of the heavenly life, and imparting it to them. They do not know their heavenly calling, with the all-sufficient provision for its fulfilment in them secured in the heavenly life of the Priest–King. And, as a consequence of this, they do not see the need for giving up the world, to have their life and walk in heaven.[20]

The church and Holy Communion

What we believe about the ascension of Christ also shapes what we believe about the church as his body. For those who spiritualise the ascension, the church has no presence in heaven through Christ and Christ is someone to remember only – not someone to remember and expect.[21] But if the ascension of Christ is bodily, then 'The church is marked off from the world ... by its mysterious union with the one whose life, though lived for the world, involves a genuine break from it.'[22] The

---

20 Andrew Murray, *The Holiest of All: A Commentary on the Book of Hebrews* (Springdale, PA: Whitaker House, 1996), 237, cited in Dawson, *Jesus Ascended*, 175.
21 Farrow, *Ascension and Ecclesia*, 60.
22 Farrow, *Ascension and Ecclesia*, 11.

church is a heavenly and not an earthly body because its Lord is in heaven and not (bodily, at least) on earth.

For Douglas Farrow, who became a Roman Catholic during the time that he wrote *Ascension Theology*, the Eucharist is the act in which the heavenly kingdom breaks into the worldly kingdoms, a sort of touchstone of heaven:

> Through it the King of Kings himself is present and adored. His sacramental coming, as the Apocalypse declares, is a sure and certain portent of his coming with glory to judge the quick and the dead. The celebration of the Eucharist is the means by which his heavenly session, otherwise invisible and impenetrable to man, is made visible; by which his intercessions before the Father are echoed and adumbrated on earth; by which the subjects of the rulers of this world are liberated and made subjects of the kingdom not of this world.[23]

It is not necessary to restrict Christ's presence to the Sacrament: the gathered church is his temple and he is present with his people through his Spirit and in corporate worship – including in the celebration of the Lord's Supper. The nature of Christ's presence in the Lord's Supper has been explored above in relation to the Articles of Religion and the Service of Holy Communion according to the *Book of Common Prayer*.

---

23 Farrow, *Ascension and Ecclesia*, 90.

Prayer

The presence of Jesus our great high priest gives us assurance of our standing before God, and enables us to pray to God, through Jesus. Calvin sums up the situation thus:

> When we pray to God we shall be rejected unless Jesus Christ is there in our name. Since he is there, He is our Intercessor and presents our prayers there and causes us to be answered, as if we had the privilege of saying what we have to do and to pour out our hearts before God ... Also, since Jesus Christ has entered into heaven, and He bears us there, although we are only brute beasts, and also He bears our names before God to show that he has us in His heart; we need not pray to God in doubt, but that we may be assured that our prayers will always be acceptable to Him, since we pray through Jesus Christ.[24]

Mission

The gospel is a message of good news about Jesus who is now installed as king in heaven and whose rule brings peace, forgiveness and direction.

---

24   John Calvin, 'Fourth Ascension sermon' cited in Dawson, *Jesus Ascended*, 40.

His rule brings peace

Christ brings peace because he has conquered the power of evil that is opposed to God and opposed to the good of all people. That victory was won at the cross, declared by the resurrection of Jesus and celebrated by the ascension of Christ to the right hand of God in heaven. Those who are in Christ are ultimately safe from the assaults of the evil one because we are seated with him far above all powers (Eph 1:20 and 2:6).

Christ brings peace because he has reconciled God and sinful human beings by his sacrificial death. The reconciliation is possible because the mediator and those for whom he mediates are one: 'Both the one who makes people holy and those who are made holy are of the same family' (Heb 2:11). The reconciliation was achieved when the mediator Jesus ascended into heaven to present humanity before God, where he remains as the pledge of our own welcome in heaven.

Because Christ is enthroned in heaven as king, he sends his Holy Spirit to empower his people for holy living. The Spirit enables the relationship between God and his people and he equips the church through spiritual gifts, distributed according to his will (Heb 2:4).

The shape of mission then is to announce what has been done by God through Jesus for sinners. Our part is to receive this invitation with repentance from sin and faith in Christ and his work for us. While we are called to imitate Christ, the gospel calls for a more radical faith in Christ that asks him to do what we cannot: to make peace with God through his blood. The ascension assures us that this peace can be made, and that it has been made.

Forgiveness and repentance will be preached in his name

Peter's sermon at Pentecost declares that the Holy Spirit was poured out *because* Jesus is exalted in heaven: 'Therefore let all Israel be assured of this: God has made this Jesus, whom you crucified, both Lord and Messiah' (Acts 2:36). Jesus' exaltation is good news for those who trust him – and very bad news for those who oppose him, which included the crowd at Pentecost. 'What shall we do,' they asked Peter (Acts 2:37), and he replied, 'Repent and be baptised, every one of you, in the name of Jesus Christ for the forgiveness of your sins. And you will receive the gift of the Holy Spirit' (Acts 2:38).

The message of Jesus' exaltation is much more than judgment for those who have opposed him; there is always the offer of forgiveness to those who repent and turn to Christ. The judge they now need to fear is also the source of the salvation that they now need to seek. He is both the king seated at the right hand of the throne of God *and* the priest seated in heaven. He intercedes on the basis of his self-offering: 'God exalted him to his own right hand as Prince and Saviour that he might bring Israel to repentance and forgive their sins' (Acts 5:31; also Acts 8:22, 10:43, 13:38, 26:18).

Christ is the lead missioner

Christ's ministry continues in heaven, even after his departure from earth. Luke–Acts is divided at the ascension of Jesus into what Jesus began to do and teach until his ascension, and what he went on to do and teach after his ascension. Jesus is still active from heaven, through the Spirit-empowered church which means that Jesus leads the mission of the church from heaven. We saw how *he* added to the number of disciples, and how *his* Spirit prevented Paul from going in one direction and opened the door to another (Acts 16:6–10), and spoke to Paul about the mission to Corinth:

> One night the Lord spoke to Paul in a vision: 'Do not be afraid; keep on speaking, do not be silent. For I am with you, and no one is going to attack and harm you, because I have many people in this city.' So Paul stayed in Corinth for a year and a half, teaching them the word of God. (Acts 18:9–11)

More implicitly, Jesus had told the disciples to 'be my witnesses in Jerusalem, and in all Judea and Samaria, and to the ends of the earth' (Acts 1:8) but the impulse to spread from Jerusalem came from the Lord. The church was scattered because of persecution (Acts 8:1), not as the result of a missionary conference; Saul was converted and commissioned as apostle to the Gentiles by the Lord, not through a missionary discernment process; Peter was persuaded to speak the gospel to Gentiles as the result of the Spirit speaking to him through a dream (Acts 10). The risen and ascended Lord directed the mission of the church in Acts and he directs the mission of the church today. It has been said that 'mission is finding out what God is doing and joining in'. In light of the ascension, we can say that God is proclaiming forgiveness through Jesus and mission is finding out how he is doing that, and where.

Christ empowers the church

Christ not only leads the mission of the church, he enables it. The mission of the Christian church begins at Pentecost as God's sons and daughters are equipped by the Holy Spirit to tell the wonders of God (Acts 2:11).

Christ equips the church through the gift of 'the apostles, the prophets, the evangelists, the pastors and teachers, to equip his people for works of service, so that the body of Christ may be built up' (Eph 4:11–12). The gifts of the Spirit cannot be separated from Christ because 'There are different kinds of gifts, but the same Spirit distributes them. There are different kinds of service, but the same Lord. There are different kinds of working, but in all of them and in everyone it is the same God at work' (1 Cor 12:4–6). The different members of the body are differently gifted by the Spirit, whom Christ poured out, for the common good (1 Cor 12:7, see also Rom 12:3–8).

The Spirit is given *because* Christ is ascended and exalted in heaven.

A surprising application: compassion

A surprising application to mission flowing from the exaltation of Christ follows from his exaltation as man. In Colossians 3:1, Paul urges Christians to set their hearts on things above where Christ is seated. As we saw above ('Worship') this means remembering that heaven is our home when we are in Christ, and renouncing this world's claims on our affections, which is described in Colossians 3:5–11. We are then exhorted to 'adorn our lives according to our identity in Christ'.[25]

---

25 Dawson, *Jesus Ascended*, 177.

This involves clothing ourselves with 'compassion, kindness, humility, gentleness and patience' and so on (Col 3:12–17). In the days of his earthly ministry, Jesus showed compassion to all, both poor and rich. He retains the flesh in which he walked the earth and showed that compassion. If then we are to clothe ourselves with adornment fitting our identity in Christ it must include sharing his compassion:

> Our union with Christ–man is strengthened when we love him by loving his poor. Because the Son of God walked among us in flesh that he yet retains, he has established the worth of all flesh. ... Moreover, he articulated the link between loving action and spiritual ascent. They are to be inseparable.[26]

Mission is not less than sharing Christ's compassion for the poor. We strengthen our union with Christ *in heaven* by care for his children *on earth*.

Preaching

It follows from what has been said above that preaching is speaking on behalf of the ascended Christ. We are the ambassadors and heralds of the king who has entrusted his message to us. We are not at liberty to alter or adulterate the message.

One of the clearest ways that we can express our desire to be faithful to God as our Principal in preaching is through sequential expository preaching in which the text rather than the preacher chooses the theme and

---

26 Dawson, *Jesus Ascended*, 178.

topic of the sermon. The Bible has been written in books (despite the constant human tendency to rearrange it into lectionaries) and by preaching through the Bible in books we can be surer of remaining faithful to its purpose and intention.[27] Expository preaching is at its best in understanding passages within their contexts. The challenge when it comes to preaching the ascension is that while it is mentioned throughout the New Testament, there are few sustained treatments of the topic that parallel the treatment of justification by faith in Romans 1–4, or the resurrection in 1 Corinthians 15. The obvious exception is the book of Hebrews but that is so much longer that it is very possible to lose sight of the ascension in the midst of the many other wonderful doctrines in that book. Elsewhere the ascension is *present* but not necessarily *primary*. How can this doctrine be preached if in most passages that mention it, the main thrust lies with a different point?

I hope that I have made the case that the ascension is a truth that should not be neglected in the church. I hope also that I have shown the ascension to be woven into the fabric of the New Testament. We have admitted that (with the exception of Hebrews), the ascension is rarely the *main* thrust of a passage. How then can it be proclaimed in an expository ministry? I can suggest the following:

- It is possible and legitimate to preach occasional doctrinal sermons without compromising one's commitment to expository ministry. In

---

27 For two short guides to expository preaching see Allan Chapple, *Preaching: A Guidebook for Beginners* (London: Latimer Trust, 2013); Ed Moll, *Stories That Serve: Using Illustrations in Expository Preaching* (Langham Publishing, 2022).

fact, it may be more honest to do so because all preachers are working from a theological system, whether they acknowledge it or not. Application often draws on theology to enrich biblical study. Topical sermons can be preached in a way that demonstrates faithful use of the texts selected in the course of the treatment. A topical sermon or series on the ascension can be preached without undermining an expository ministry. I would argue instead that it will enrich an expository ministry by illuminating and informing those places where the ascension is mentioned apparently in passing, but in fact as a foundation.

- Dawson argues that 'The doctrine of the ascension keeps us from collapsing our understanding of the person of Christ into any of the Christological distortions of the present age.'[28] If we accept his point, then a doctrinal sermon or series on the ascension would be good medicine (or, perhaps more accurately, vitamins and minerals) to prevent spiritual ill-health in the church.

- It is also possible and legitimate, from time to time, to major on a minor note in a passage. I would argue that main points *must* be made and that minor points *may* be made. If the ascension is a minor note in a passage, it can be mentioned. We saw, for example, that while Article 4 is nominally about the resurrection, the ascension is a significant minor note. One practical option is to pause a sequential preaching series to reflect on a theme that has been raised in the text and

---

28 Dawson, *Jesus Ascended*, 91.

make connections within the book. An example of 'coming up for air' in this way might be to pause and reflect on Ephesians 1:20–21 in light of the whole epistle.

• The ascension informs our practice of worship and of ministry: it should underlie the words that we sing and pray. In the church I serve, we work hard to ensure that the words we sing reinforce the gospel that we believe, including the ascension of Christ.

However we do it, let us not neglect the doctrine of the ascension, but instead let us follow the disciples who worshipped the ascended Lord with great joy (Luke 24:52).

Appendix: Preaching Illustrations

The following is not an exhaustive collection to illustrate every aspect of the ascension but they are offered here as a resource.

The Stone of Scone

In 1996, a piece of rock was moved from England to Scotland. It is an oblong block of red sandstone, about 26 inches (660 mm) by 16 inches (410 mm) by 10.5 inches (270 mm) in size and weighing approximately 336 pounds (152 kg). The top bears chisel-marks. At each end of the stone is an iron ring, apparently intended to make transport easier.

Why was this transfer a major news item? Not because moving a rock is such a big deal (rocks are moved all the time), but because of what the rock represented: the rock is the Stone of Scone which was used for centuries in the coronation of the monarchs of Scotland. In 1296, the Stone was captured by Edward I of England as spoils of war and taken to Westminster Abbey in London, where it was fitted into a wooden chair, known as St. Edward's Chair, on which all subsequent English sovereigns except Queen Mary I and Queen Mary II have been crowned.

The return of the Stone to Scotland represents a return of sovereignty to Scotland. It is symbolic because, despite devolved government, Scotland is still part of the United Kingdom (and has been since the Union in 1707). But for independence-minded Scots, the transfer of the Stone of Scone from London to Scotland is significant.

Comment: This story could be used to make the point that in the ascension Jesus was not retiring as king but returning to exercise that dominion from his rightful throne.

Serving the Ascended King (Hugh Latimer)

Hugh Latimer (about 1485–1555) was an English Bishop and Reformer, and also a very bold preacher. One day he preached before Henry VIII, who was offended by what he considered to be a lack of respect to the king's majesty. The king ordered him to preach again on the following Sunday to make up for it.

Latimer began his sermon thus:

> Hugh Latimer, do you know before whom you are to speak today? To the high and mighty monarch, the king's most excellent majesty, who can take away thy life, if you cause offence. Therefore, take heed that you speak not a word that may displease. But then consider well, Hugh, do you not know where you came from – on whose account you are sent? By the great and mighty God, Who is all-present and Who sees all your ways and Who is able to cast your soul into hell! Therefore, take care that you deliver your message faithfully.

Latimer then proceeded to deliver the very same sermon which he had given the preceding week – with considerably more enthusiasm! He did so because he knew that above the monarch before him sat a greater king, the ascended Christ in heaven.[29]

Comment: One implication of Christ's kingship is that he demands our ultimate loyalty, above even that of our highest earthly rulers.

The Yellow Ribbon Tree

There's a story of a young man from an honest, hardworking and proud family. He was returning home after a year away, travelling by bus. The old lady in the next seat asked him whether he was looking forward to being home. 'I'm not sure,' he said, 'I don't know that I *am* going home.'

He explained that he had spent the last year in prison; he was deeply ashamed – for himself and for his family. Just before his release he had written to his mother: 'I am coming out of prison next week. I'll take the bus that goes through [the town he grew up in]. I understand that you may never want to see me again, and if that's so, I'll just stay on the bus. If you will see me again, even just once, tie a ribbon to the tree outside our house. As the bus goes past, I'll know whether to stay on or to get off.'

The old lady said, 'I'll look out the window with you, just to make sure you don't miss the ribbon.' When the bus came to pass the tree, they could hardly miss the sign; every branch on the tree was covered in ribbons.

Those ribbons were a statement of his welcome home. We can imagine that as he walked home from the bus stop, he simply kept his eyes on those ribbons, even as

---

29 I have not found an original source for this. The tale is told in http://www.romans45.org/spurgeon/misc/ep04.htm (accessed 15 August 2024).

his heart was in his boots. The ribbons proclaimed that he had been forgiven and was welcome here.

Comment: We look to Jesus, seated at the right hand: every time we see him, seated at the right hand, we know that we are forgiven and we are welcome there, 'fixing our eyes on Jesus, the pioneer and perfecter of faith. For the joy set before him he endured the cross, scorning its shame, and sat down at the right hand of the throne of God' (Heb 12:2).

John Calvin's comment on the work of the ascended Christ is also apposite:

> He so reconciles the Father's heart to us that by his intercession he prepares a way and access for us to the Father's throne. He fills with grace and kindness the throne that for miserable sinners would otherwise have been filled with dread.[30]

The Coronation Gift (Archelaus)

We are used to coronations taking place in our midst and certainly within the country being ruled. In ancient times it was not unknown for someone to go away to be made king by a higher ruler. Jesus mentions this as the background to a parable when he says, 'A man of noble birth went to a distant country to have himself appointed king and then to return' (Luke 19:12). He likely had in mind that when King Herod died in 4 BC, his son Archelaus went away to be made king in his place.

---

30   Calvin, *Institutes*, 2.16.16.

Imagine that you were waiting in Judea as part of 'Team Archelaus': how would you know whether he had been made king? Communications were slow (no phone or email!) and the new king might be delayed for some time in Rome with his new duties. The sign of a successful trip would come with the first boat to bring gifts from the new king in Rome. The coronation gifts are evidence that 'your man' has been made king. And the greater the king the greater the gift of course. (It so happens that Archelaus was not successful in his bid to become king.)

The heart of Peter's sermon on the Day of Pentecost in Acts 2 is that giving of the Spirit is the visible gift that tells us of Jesus' invisible coronation in heaven. 'News of this coronation in heaven (still hidden from view) has reached earth in the pandemonium of Pentecost.'[31]

Comment: Peter's Pentecost sermon is evidence of Christ's enthronement in heaven.

Drake's folly (oil)

In 1859, at Titusville, Pennsylvania, an event occurred which changed the face of modern life. It is no exaggeration to say that almost every facet of daily life in the modern world depends on what happened in 1859. We don't remember or celebrate the event, but we depend on the fruits every day.

According to the State of Louisiana, in 1859 Colonel Edwin Drake drilled the first successful well through rock and produced crude oil.[32] What some called

---

31 Farrow, *Ascension and Ecclesia*, 25.
32 https://www.dnr.louisiana.gov/assets/tad/education/bgbb/2/ancient_use.html (Accessed 16 November 2024).

'Drake's Folly' was the birth of the modern petroleum industry. He sold his 'black gold' for $20 a barrel.

We don't remember Colonel Drake or 1859 with any kind of celebration. But we depend on oil, plastics and many other petroleum products all the time. We simply could not imagine a world without the petroleum industry.

Comment: Whether or not we celebrate the ascent of Christ to heaven, we depend on the fruits of his ascent every day of our Christian lives.

COBRA is on the move

The UK Government's emergency response committee is known as COBRA, after the place where it meets (Cabinet Office Briefing Room A). In the disaster movie *Flood*, London is under threat from a flood and the government must move or be overwhelmed.[33] The COBRA committee is moved to High Wycombe outside London and continues to direct the government's response from there. Despite no longer meeting in the room of that name, the committee is still referred to as COBRA.

Comment: In the ascension, Jesus did not retire. He still directs the church but now from a new 'location'. The weakness of this illustration is that COBRA's move is a simple translation of activities whereas Jesus' ascension creates something new: see 'Cosmology'.

Over to you!

I was chatting to another minister about how to preach on the ascension of Christ and he told me what he

---

33   Directed by Tony Mitchell (Lionsgate, 2007).

had done. Having declared (from the pulpit) that Jesus left his disciples when he ascended into heaven, the minister immediately proceeded to leave the congregation by exiting the church building. He went home to the vicarage and did not return to church at all that day.

At the first the congregation were too stunned to react. After a few moments, though, some of the key movers and shakers got something going and the service continued in a manner of speaking. They muddled on without him and without any direction from him.

He thought that this was a brilliant illustration of the ascension of Christ who departed this earth and left the disciples to get on without him.

Comment: This is clearly not what the New Testament teaches about the ascension of Christ. But it is terrifyingly close to what many believe, including those who spiritualise the ascension, whether or not they have heard of Origen, Schleiermacher or Hegel.

A single movement: Rugby union

In Rugby Union, a try is scored when the ball is grounded behind the try-line. Sometimes a player is tackled and brought to ground before the try-line. They can still score if either (a) the player's momentum carries them in a continuous movement along the ground into the opponents' in-goal or (b) the player is tackled near to the opponents' goal line and the player immediately reaches out and grounds the ball. It *looks* like two movements but in fact it is a single movement with two steps. The resurrection and ascension are two steps but they form a single movement.

Comment: The illustration depends on a knowledge of the rules of Rugby Union, on which even some players are confused!

Select bibliography

Introductory

F. F. Bruce, *Jesus: Past, Present and Future* (Eastbourne: Kingsway, 1998).

B. K. Donne, *Christ Ascended* (Exeter: Paternoster Press, 1983).

Douglas Farrow, *Ascension Theology* (London: Bloomsbury Publishing, 2011).

Patrick Schreiner, *The Ascension of Christ: Recovering a Neglected Doctrine* (Bellingham, WA: Lexham Press, 2020).

More substantial

Gerrit Scott Dawson, *Jesus Ascended: The Meaning of Christ's Continuing Incarnation* (London: T&T Clark International, 2004).

Douglas Farrow, *Ascension and Ecclesia: On the Significance of the Ascension for Ecclesiology and Christian Cosmology* (Edinburgh, T&T Clark Ltd, 1999).

Peter Orr, *Exalted Above the Heavens: The Risen and Ascended Christ* (London: Apollos, 2018).

Alan J. Thompson, *The Acts of the Risen Lord Jesus* (London: Apollos, 2011).

In our Latimer Studies series

What can be learned from Thomas Cranmer's theology of the Trinity, and why does it merit closer examination? This book considers Cranmer's Trinitarian theology from various angles, drawing on his writings, including the 1553 Articles of Faith and the 1552 Book of Common Prayer. It explores his theological debt to the Church Fathers, fellow Reformers, and Medieval theology, demonstrating how Cranmer articulated a fully historic, orthodox, and Reformed doctrine of the Trinity. Rather than leaving behind a comprehensive theological treatise, Cranmer's greatest achievement was imprinting the realities of the triune Godhead in the hearts and minds of the English-speaking world through his liturgy.

The book concludes with reflections on Cranmer's Trinitarian legacy, noting his influence on subsequent generations of Anglicans and addressing contemporary concerns in Trinitarian theology, seeking enduring insights from Cranmer's work. It aims to encourage us to follow Cranmer's lead in knowing, trusting and delighting in Father, Son and Holy Spirit.

Also in our Christian Doctrine series

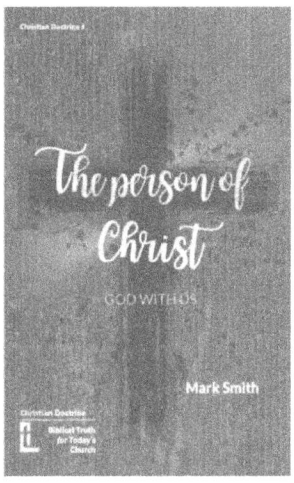

In this short and stimulating guide to the doctrine of the Person of Christ, Mark Smith explores the biblical witness to Jesus as both fully God and fully man. He shows how these truths were articulated and defended in the debates of the early church, and why they remain deeply relevant to the lives of Christians today.

The second half of the book then dives into the Christological content of the Anglican formularies (the Thirty-Nine Articles of Religion and the Book of Common Prayer). Here we discover how the Church of England possesses a rich storehouse of reflection on the identity of Jesus Christ – not only as a doctrine to be understood, but as a person to be worshipped and adored.

In our St Antholin lecture series

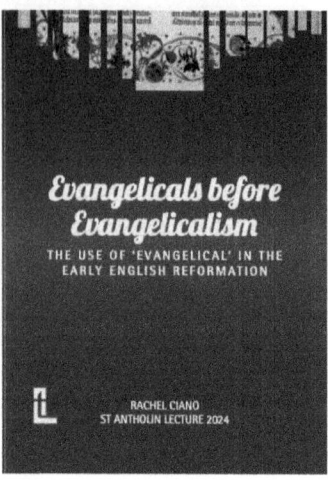

Rachel Ciano examines the early use of the term 'evangelical' during the English Reformation, long before the rise of modern Evangelicalism. Focusing on the Henrician and Edwardian periods, Ciano highlights how 'evangelical' became a key identifier for reformers embracing justification by faith alone, clerical marriage, and scriptural authority. She offers a fresh perspective on the development of evangelical identity and its role in shaping England's religious landscape in the sixteenth century.

www.ingramcontent.com/pod-product-compliance
Lightning Source LLC
Chambersburg PA
CBHW051657040426
42446CB00009B/1172